COACHING FOOTBALL'S TILTED-NOSE TECHNIQUE

Denny Marcin
James A. Peterson

COACHES CHOICE

ISBN: 1-57167-090-4
Library of Congress Catalog Card Number: 96-71931

Book Layout and Diagrams: Antonio J. Perez
Cover Design: Deborah M. Bellaire

Coaches Choice Books is an imprint of: Sagamore Publishing, Inc.
P.O. Box 647
Champaign, IL 61824-0647
(800) 327-5557
(217) 359-5940
Fax: (217) 359-5975
Web Site: http//www.sagamorepub.com

DEDICATION

I'd like to dedicate this book to my wife Betsey, sons—Jeff and Denny, daughter-in-law Lynn, daughters—Melinda and Susan, and grandson Carlton. Without their encouragement and love I couldn't have accomplished the many things I have done in my career.

I hope you enjoy the book as much as I did writing it.

Part of the proceeds from the sales of this book will be donated to the American Heart Association.

D.M.

ACKNOWLEDGMENTS

The authors are grateful to Susie Goldner for typing the manuscript. In addition, we also appreciate the invaluable assistance provided by the staff at Sagamore Publishing Company—particularly Antonio Perez and Deborah Bellaire. Also, we would like to thank Beth and Mark Jones for the use of their photos. Finally, we would to thank Dr. Gary Miller for his efforts in the early stages of the project.

CONTENTS

Chapter

PREFACE

In my 33 years of coaching football at the high school and college level, I've concluded that the margin between those teams which achieve the highest levels of success and those with comparable talent but who fail for whatever reason to prosper is often relatively slim. While many factors can affect the degree to which a football team is able to be successful (e.g., talent, coaching, conditioning, the will to win, the ability level of its opponents, etc.), one of the most important elements of success is the defensive system the team employs. An appropriate defensive system is one which enables a team to make the most effective use of its personnel, while simultaneously allowing it to effectively defend against the strengths of its opponents.

Regardless of which defense a team uses, there are defensive techniques which can enhance the effectiveness of that defensive system. The tilted-nose is such a technique. Because the tilted-nose provides the front defenders with an exceptional scheme to read the play, react to specific keys, and get to the ball, the defense is given an extraordinary opportunity to control the tempo of the game.

I wrote this book to provide coaches at all competitive levels a tool that can enable them to make maximum use of the skills and attributes of their players. *Coaching Football's Tilted-Nose Technique* offers step-by-step instructions on how to install the tilted-nose and how to use this uniquely effective method as a cornerstone to build defensive fronts and stunts to defend against a wide array of offensive situations. The book also features chapters on playing off blocks, tackling fundamentals, pass rushing fundamentals, and movement fundamentals.

I firmly believe that every coach can benefit from the methods and advice presented in this book. If in the process of utilizing the information offered in this book coaches are better able to achieve their professional goals, then the efforts to write *Coaching Football's Tilted-Nose Technique* will have been worthwhile.

Denny Marcin

CHAPTER 1

Tough Enough to Play
the Tilted-Nose Technique

One of the most fundamental and indisputable axioms related to football is the fact that tough teams have tough defenses. Not surprisingly, such defenses do not happen by accident. Rather, a tough defense is the by-product of the efforts of a well-prepared, well-organized staff of coaches who are working with players who have certain athletic abilities, an indomitable will-to-win, and a task-oriented commitment to the job at hand.

As a general rule, no group of defenders tends to be tougher or play a more critical role in determining the collective mindset of a team's defense than defensive linemen. Often referred to as a "special breed", defensive linemen are usually at the core of a tough defense. The nose guard, for example, is the pivotal point of a defense that utilizes the tilted-nose technique. Not only is he typically the leading tackler up front, he also plays a critical role in keeping the center off the linebackers.

As a point of fact, defensive linemen typically possess certain characteristics and certain skills. Accordingly, coaches who want to ensure that their teams play tough defense should select defensive linemen who exhibit these characteristics and have these skills.

Desirable Characteristics

* *Physical.* Because of the uniqueness of the nose guard position in the tilted-nose technique, some physical characteristics are more important than others. A quicker, more agile type of player with good upper body strength is required at the nose. Height is not a primary concern at this position. Typically, players over 6'3" are not as quick as the shorter players, and are therefore less appealing candidates for the nose position. At the Division 1 level, nose guards should weigh anywhere between 255 and 285 pounds. Wrestler types with good quickness and exceptional upper body strength are ideal candidates. All factors considered, quickness is more important than foot speed at this position. The nose guard must be proficient at making plays off the ground as well as on his feet. Strength is important in pressing the line of scrimmage and keeping the center off of the linebackers.

- *Enthusiastic.* Defensive lineman—particularly the nose guard in the tilted-nose technique—must play with a zeal that enables them to give 100% on every play. Such a fervor should enhance the likelihood that they are a constant force that the offensive line must reckon with.

- *Intimidating.* Intimidation can be a frightening factor. Defensive linemen who intimidate their opponents have several advantages—not the least of which is their ability to force their opponents to unduly focus on them rather than on their assigned responsibilities.

- *Aggressive.* All factors considered, football is a battle between two groups of warriors. Defensive linemen should view their gridiron role as aggressors who are defending their turf with all the energy and controlled passion at their disposal. In other words, play with reckless abandon ...attack... disengage... win.

- *Productive.* Regardless of what characteristics a player possesses, the bottom line is that he must be able to do his job in a productive manner. Successful defensive schemes are the collective by-product of several defenders working together to achieve a common goal. A defender who does not produce on the field may compromise the efforts of the other ten defenders.

Requisite Skills
- *Strike.* Defenders must be able to strike a blow (i.e., hit) at a blocker. The strike must be performed on the rise with the heel of a defender's hands, his thumbs rolled to a twelve o'clock position. Hand speed is critical. It is important that a defender is able to get his hands out of his stance and get them up as quickly as possible. Keep in mind that the primary objective is to strike a forceful blow, rather than push on the defender (a very common mistake made at both the high school and college level).

- *Read.* Defenders (particularly those who play in a read defense as opposed to a pressure defense) must be able to read their assigned visual keys. Defenders in a read defense—other than the nose guard in the tilted-nose position— should be back off the football approximately two feet. Keep in mind that the ability to read is an acquired skill that takes some time to develop. Accordingly, inexperienced defenders may require some time to develop. As the ability to read is refined, a defender can move slightly closer to the L.O.S..

- *React.* Defenders must be able to not only read their visual keys, but to react to them. The ability to physically and mentally respond to a specific stimulus is a critical factor in being able to be in the right place at the right time.

- *Re-react.* Football is a dynamic, fluid game. A defender must be able to re-react to events as they are occurring. A defender responds to a key. His opponent reacts to his response. Concurrently, the offensive player with the ball must respond to events as they are evolving. Through all of this, the defender must react instantaneously to circumstances.

- *Get off the block.* Defenders must be able to shed blockers. The defender's objective is to get to the man with the ball. The offensive blocker's goal is to prevent that from happening. In order to be productive, a defender must be able to get off a block and then get his nose in the action.

- *Maximum pursuit.* One of the primary goals of every sound defense must be maximum pursuit to the ball on every play. Accordingly, coaches should give their defensive players a pursuit grade on every snap. The defenders' relative effort in getting to the ball should be emphasized and evaluated on every play. Coaches should emphasize to players that not only getting to the ball, but getting their "nose in the pile" is important.

- *Sprint to the ball.* Defenders must sprint to the ball. Football is a high-action game. Defenders need to get excited about getting to the ball. Part-and-parcel of such excitement is moving to the ball with reckless abandon.

- *Gang tackle.* No defender should ever just watch a play or give up on a play. Gang tackling helps to build the defensive team's morale and to raise the productivity of the defense, while punishing the offensive ball carrier and causing turnovers.

- *Get excited on every play.* Defensive players should relish the opportunity to play football—each and every play. A mindset that reflects a defender's unabashed appetite for playing will enhance his ability to get the job done.

CHAPTER 2

Understanding the
Tilted-Nose Technique

What Is the Tilted-Nose?

The tilted-nose is a defensive technique in which the nose guard is aligned at a 45-degree angle on the center. The tilted-nose is a very effective technique that can be employed from a variety of defenses (refer to Chapter 5 for additional information on the basic fronts in which the tilted-nose technique can be used).

Successfully utilized to defend against both running and passing situations, the tilted-nose offers a number of advantages as a defensive technique, including:

• It provides the nose guard with a significant advantage for defeating the center's reach block (one of the most popular blocks currently used in football). In fact, in many situations, the tilted-nose technique will actually cause a team to eliminate its reach block scheme to the tilted-nose side.

• By reading the farside guard, the nose guard can determine on the farside guard's first step what type of play he is going to get and whether he is on the frontside or the backside. For example, if the farside guard pulls toward the nose guard one step, the nose guard should immediately realize that the guard on his backside (the onside guard) is going to block down on him and that he is on the frontside counter play (a play that most teams run today).

• By reading the farside guard, the nose guard can readily recognize when a pass play is called. His recognition enables the defense to adjust the actions of the 5-technique tackle (the tackle who is lined up over the outside edge of the offensive tackle to the tilted-nose side) to improve the defensive coverage against the play that was called. For example, if the defense called involves bringing the five technique on a slant move inside the offensive tackle, the nose who is reading his visual key can be brought all the way around the 5-technique to act as the contain player on a passing play. As a result, the defensive team doesn't have to expend (i.e., waste) a linebacker on any kind of contain responsibility. The nose guard serves as the contain defender.

- It provides the nose guard with an advantage in defeating the scoop block on his backside—in this case by the onside guard. If the center attempts to reach block away from the nose, the nose guard should recognize that someone will likely try to scoop block him from the backside and react accordingly.

How the Tilted-Nose Can Help a Team

The tilted-nose technique can enable a team to make maximum use of the skills and attributes of its players. Because its visual and pressure keys are so exceptionally accurate, the tilted-nose defense provides the front defenders with an enhanced opportunity to read the play, react to the keys, and get to the ball. The better the defenders are able to read their keys the more likely they will be able to out-execute their opponents. Being able to recognize the type of offensive play that was called and which direction it is being run gives defenders a substantial advantage over the offensive team. Certain blocking schemes become more difficult to perform—if not impossible. Stunting options are increased. Access to the ball carrier often is facilitated by the accuracy of the read-and-react features of the tilted-nose. Coordination between the various defenders is enhanced. As a result, collectively the tilted-nose allows the defense to control the tempo of the game. The ability to control an opponent's offense is the fundamental factor both in sound defense and in winning.

CHAPTER 3

Installing the Tilted-Nose

Installing the tilted-nose technique requires that the coach consider several fundamental philosophical issues. First, the noseguard should be recognized as the pivotal position of the defense. He is a key player because of his job description. He must keep the center off the linebackers, thereby enabling them to have relatively unimpeded access to go where they need to go during a play. The nose will most likely be the leading tackler of the front personnel, and in most cases the leading tackler for losses, since he is the front player closest to the football.

When installing the defensive scheme, the ability of the nose to have a "three-way go" should be maintained. A "three-way go" means the nose can do one of three things: play straight, go inside a player, or go outside a player. By presenting the possibility of the three-way go and by flipping defenders, the defensive team may now create the mismatches they desire with the offensive personnel.

Second, the coach should recognize that the tilted-nose takes a good amount of teaching technique to master and accordingly should not be approached as a "part-time" technique. A visual key and a pressure key must be taught for each of the eight basic blocking schemes that a tilted-nose is going to see. Reading the far guard is the primary key to success in the tilted-nose. Although the nose is taught a three-way go, his key never changes. A commitment to master the eight basic blocking schemes should be made before any change ups are considered. An overview of the guidelines for how the noseguard, 3 technique, and 5 technique should read and respond to the blocking schemes is presented in Chapter 4.

When installing the tilted-nose technique, the coach should assume his players know practically nothing about this technique, even if they have been exposed to this particular defensive technique previously. As a result, when teaching the tilted-nose, a coach should start from square one, with a logical, complete teaching progression. He should also use and present teaching terms and ideas in ways players will make sense of and remember. This can significantly simplify the installation of the tilted-nose. For example, most players tend to remember terms or rules that rhyme. One illustration of applying such a concept to a defensive rule would be: "tackle pulls away, bootleg your way." Coaches should present concepts in a way that involves no more than three ideas at a time. Players typically cannot process more information than three ideas (if that) at once. For example, in teaching tackling, the three basic points that could be emphasized to defenders would be: (1) attack, (2) chest on chest, (3) rip your arms up. Keep in mind that overloading a player's ability to process information will inevitably hinder the learning process for a player and raise the likelihood that mistakes might be made. The important point is "don't take a good player and make him a robot."

Lastly, and perhaps most critical, is the consideration of the physical, mental, and attitudinal characteristics the nose must possess. A coach should take advantage of and structure his team's defensive scheme around the strengths of his players. Regardless of the quantity or quality of instruction, if the nose does not possess the requisite skills and characteristics attendant of the position, the success level of the defensive scheme is most likely to be compromised.

Selecting a Nose Guard

Since the nose guard is a pivotal player in the defensive front for the tilted-nose technique, it is critical that he possess certain characteristics and specific skills. An overview of these characteristics and skills was presented in Chapter 1. The coach should keep in mind that the "perfect" nose guard rarely exists. As a result, the coach should realize that it is important to identify the specific and particular strengths of any one nose guard and structure the defensive schemes to be used accordingly. All players have strengths and weaknesses. A coach should always attempt to take advantage of the things a particular defender—in this case, the nose—can do well.

Stance and Alignment

The stance and alignment are as critical as anything that is discussed in this book. The nose guard in the tilted-nose technique should assume a three-point stance, the hand nearest the ball is down and his inside foot is back. The far hand is up, palm facing the center, ready to strike the near shoulder of the center if he reach blocks. It is important for the stance to be comfortable. The head of the nose guard should be in a comfortable (rather than strained) position. The nose guard's feet should be approximately shoulder-width apart, although this may vary with each individual according to what is comfortable and what he is asked to do. His knees should be facing the same direction as his toes. His weight should be on his up foot because his first step should be with his back foot. Because we flip sides of the football, we must be proficient at both a right- and left-handed stance. A right-handed stance means we align with our right hand on the ground and our right foot back. The coach should use terms "up foot and back foot," not right and left when referring to stance.

The nose guard aligns tilted in an almost ear-to-ear relationship on the center. It is absolutely essential that the nose guard aligns in a 45-degree angle as he faces the offensive center, making sure that his down hand is between the ball and the near foot of the center (Diagram 3-1 and Photos 3-1 to 3-5). He should get as much of the ball as possible, but no part of his body should be past the ball. His depth of alignment is dependent upon his being able to see his visual key—the far guard. As a general rule, the nose should try to crowd the ball as long as he can see his visual key. If the visual key is "is back", he must move back accordingly. The down hand should be in a tripod position with the weight on his fingertips, not his knuckles. As a result, the nose can spring out of his stance quicker.

Correct mechanics for the right-handed stance in the tilted-nose technique.

Photo 3-1
Top view.

Photo 3-2
Top/side view.

Photo 3-3
Ground level view.

Photo 3-4
Visual key view.

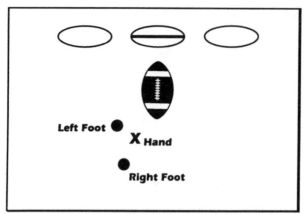

Diagram 3-1

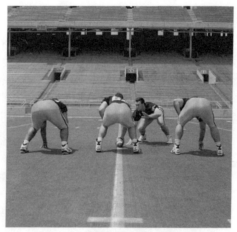

Photo 3-5
View from behind the offense.

How to Avoid Common Mistakes in the Tilted-Nose

The proper mechanics (e.g., alignment, stance, movement, etc.) for the tilted-nose were discussed and illustrated in detail in the previous section of this chapter. Not surprisingly, a nose guard who compromises his adherence to those mechanics diminishes his level of effectiveness. Accordingly, coaches who adopt the tilted-nose must constantly emphasize the importance of strictly adhering to the "right way" to do things. Among the more common mistakes in the tilted-nose are the following:

• The nose may be tilted too much (i.e., greater than the prescribed 45-degree angle). In other words, his tail end is toward the line of scrimmage too much, away from the 45-degree angle. This mistake gives the nose too flat a course down the line of scrimmage.

- The nose is not tilted enough. This mistake puts him back into a shaded position, which defeats several of the purposes of tilting the nose in the first place—particularly, avoiding the reach block by the center. This error may also hinder the nose's ability to clearly see his visual key.

- The nose is too far off the ball. This mistake inhibits the ability of the nose to crowd the center and to keep him off the linebackers. The coach wants the nose to attack the center—not avoid him.

- The nose doesn't have his off hand up in the air, ready to strike a blow. The tilted-nose is a hitting defense. This mistake hinders the ability of the nose to control the blocker.

- The nose, while coming out of his stance, doesn't take a step, rather he just lunges forward and places his hands on the center. This mistake puts the nose in a position where he can't react properly to his read. By failing to control the center and getting into a squared-up position where he is ready (and able) to move as his read dictates, the nose greatly diminishes his effectiveness. In this instance, the nose is mistakenly trying to get by solely on his upper-body strength. While upper-body strength is important, it is a poor substitute for being in the right place at the right time.

- The nose takes too big of a first step. This mistake often causes the nose to be off balance. As a result, he can't change directions very well.

Incorrect mechanics for the right-handed stance in the tilted-nose technique.

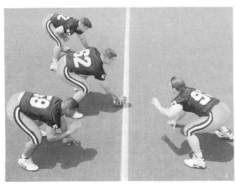

Photo 3-6
Too far off the football.

Photo 3-7
Not tilted at a 45-degree angle.

Photo 3-8
Too far across the football.

- The nose makes his first step with the wrong foot (particularly against a reach block). For whatever reason, some players want to punch and step with the up foot, instead of stepping with the back foot. In this instance, the nose loses much of his leverage for striking a blow and unduly widens his base position, which, in turn, compromises his ability to move (redirect) effectively.

Keys and Responsibilities

The tilted-nose technique is employed most often in a reading defense. The visual key of the nose guard is critical. He must read the far guard, not the center. This factor may be the most important point in terms of the tilted-nose guard technique. The nose's visual key is the head gear of the far guard. He should not have to turn his head to read his key. The reason we read the far guard and not the center is that we get a "quicker read" which enables us to react quicker. Diagram 3-2 illustrates eight of the blocks that the nose's visual key gives him. At the least, the farside guard's first step lets the nose know if the play called is to the nose's frontside or backside.

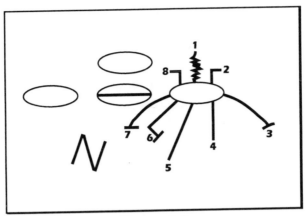

Diagram 3-2

1. Pass/Draw
2. Backside- Pull
3. Backside- Reach
4. Backside/Frontside- Base
5. Backside- Runs thru
6. Frontside- Fan
7. Frontside- Scoop
8. Frontside- Pull

The tilted-nose's pressure key is the offensive guard on the side of the nose (Diagram 3-3). In reality, the onside guard cannot be seen, he must be felt. Accordingly, the tilted-nose should never be reach blocked by the center and should be able to successfully defeat the scoop block by the guard (pressure key).

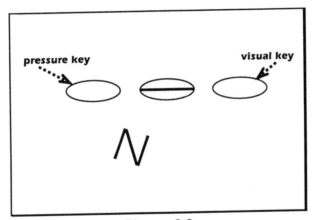

Diagram 3-3

Depending on his initial read, the nose guard's responsibility versus run action to his side is the 1 gap. On run action away from the nose guard, he squeezes the center to the far 1 gap. He must keep the center off the linebackers. In passing situations, the nose rushes the 1 gap in which he is aligned.

Initial Movement and Strike Blow

In any reading defense, the first step of the defender is critical. Any movement of the ball initiates the nose guard's first step. He should step with his inside foot with a straight ahead step that could be as short as six inches or as much as one stride, depending on his visual key. He should have the ability to read his visual keys as his first step is coming down so that the second step will be in the proper direction. As he moves, the nose should strike a blow with both hands on the center. The strike should be on the rise, delivering the blow with the heel of his hands, with his thumbs rolling to twelve o'clock (which helps keep his elbows in). Coaches should emphasize to the nose that this blow is a strike—a punch, not a push.

Drill 3-1: Quick Hands Drill

Objective: To teach and practice raising the hands quickly to get them into a striking position.

Equipment needed: Stop watch

Discussion: Defensive linemen (D) stand with their hands at their sides and form two lines facing each other (C). The coach stands in front of the players with a stopwatch. On the coach's command, the players are given ten seconds to see how many times they can get their hands up to a striking position. One line will go first and their partners should count.

Coaching points:
- Encourage quickness
- Lead with heels of hands
- Roll thumbs to twelve o'clock while striking
- Keep track of improvement
- Good off-season drill

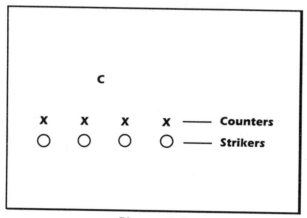

Diagram 3-4

CHAPTER 4

Playing Off Blocks

As a general rule, defensive linemen must fight off blockers on every play. One of the critical factors in this regard is that each defender must believe that his particular area of responsibility is the most important area in the team's coordinated defense. Accordingly, although a defender may be "blocked" at times, he must not stay blocked.

After contact is made, a defender has several ways to get to the ball carrier or the quarterback. Four of the more commonly used techniques that defensive linemen utilize to fight off blocks are the "read", "pressure", "rip", and "skin". In the "read" technique, the defensive lineman delivers a blow to the chest of the offensive lineman and then separates and sprints to the ball. In the "pressure" technique, the defender attempts to penetrate the offensive line so that he can get behind the line of scrimmage and into the backfield. The defender who uses a "rip" technique (in which he throws his outside arm across the body of the offensive lineman blocking him) with a quick lead step in order to get by his opponent and into a gap. In the "skin" technique, the defender (who is usually head up on an opponent) steps out and up with his up foot and ends up outside his visual key.

Most coaches believe that a defensive lineman should not run around a blocker. These coaches hold the opinion that in this instance, the defender becomes a chaser instead of a pursuer. In other words, he has blocked himself. In addition, when a defender runs around a blocker, he frequently opens a running lane for the ball carrier. His shoulders should stay as squared up as possible to give the defender the opportunity to make a play to either side of the blocker.

The next three sections of this chapter examine how three particular defensive linemen—the noseguard, the 3 technique, and the 5 technique—should react to a variety of basic blocking techniques, in response to specific run and pass reads.

Noseguard

- *Alignment*
  Align tilted in an ear-to-ear relationship on the center. Get as much of the ball as possible.

- *Stance*
  Assume a 3-point stance. The noseguard's inside foot is back. The noseguard's far hand is ready to strike the near shoulder if the center reaches him.

- *Key*
  The visual key is the head gear of the far guard. The noseguard's pressure key is the onside guard to his side.

- *Responsibility*
  <u>Run to</u>: the 1 gap on noseguard's side. <u>Run away</u>: squeeze the center to the far 1 gap. The noseguard must keep the center off the linebacker. <u>Pass</u>: the noseguard rushes the 1 gap in which he is aligned.

- *Movement and blow*
  Move on the football. Step six inches with the inside foot. Strike a blow with both hands on the center.

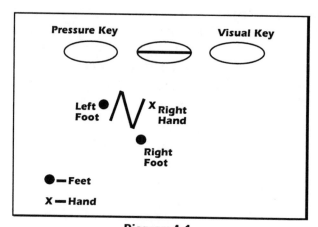

Diagram 4-1

1. Base Block
   (This block must be carefully researched in a team's scouting efforts to determine if it is a backside or a frontside block). If your read tells you that you are on the backside of a play, step with the inside foot and strike a blow with both hands on the center. The far hand should strike on the center's pectorals and the hand closest to the football should attack to the far shoulder. You are always pressing the L.O.S. as you go. Even though you are in a tilted alignment, your body should square up as you near the L.O.S. Stay on the backside of the center as long as the ball has a threat of coming back. Once your gap is secure and the ballcarrier presents no cutback threat, you should be a football player and cross the center's face and pursue.

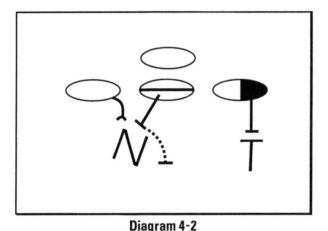

Diagram 4-2

2. Scoop Block
   (Flat course by your visual key). This could be a scramble block if your
   opponents employ that technique. A coach needs to know this information
   to help his players. Take a short six-inch step with the back foot and be
   ready to take a second step (we call this a press step) with the up foot.
   Attack the lead shoulder of the center with the up hand. You will be
   squared up on your second step. Maintain your gap control always working
   just off the mid-line of a blocker. In other words your helmet should be
   between the nose and the tip of the shoulder of the blocker. This action
   will enable you to maintain your gap and get across the blocker's face if the
   ball cuts back. If you get too far away from the blocker, you have very little
   chance to make a play on the cut back.

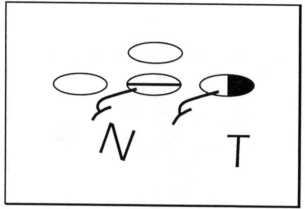

Diagram 4-3

3. Reach Block

(Any action away gives you a backside read). This read tells you that you could get scooped by the guard or you could get a combination block from the center and the guard. Either way you know the ball will start away from you. You should keep the center off the linebacker as long as possible. Step with the inside foot and press the center squeezing him to the far 1 gap and trying to turn his shoulders parallel with the L.O.S. Cross the face only when the threat of the cutback is eliminated.

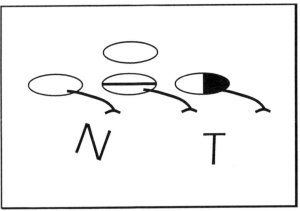

Diagram 4-4

4. Guard Pulls to You

(You are now on the frontside of a play—probably a counter or a trap). This situation is the most important reason that reading the far guard is critical. In reading the center (as most teams do), the nose guard could get hit by both the center and his pressure key, which may cause confusion as to where the ball is going. It could be a double team, a counter play or a combination block and he could be on the backside of a play. By reading his visual key, however, the nose knows that he is on the frontside of a play. The important point to remember is that the nose knows that his pressure key will block him.

If the center blocks your inside number and your pressure key blocks down on you, you should step with the inside foot and defeat the center's block first. The L.O.S. must be maintained. As the nose guard feels pressure, he should attack the 1-gap and try to get a seam. If caught, you have several options:

- As you attack the 1-gap, drive your far arm into the seam between the center and the onside guard and create a pile, while trying to maintain pressure on the center (not allowing him to get to the linebacker). You must stay under the pads of the center and the guard. You must maintain your leverage. You can drop to your knees and create a pile.

- As you attack the 1-gap, drive your far arm into the seam between the center and the guard. You now can use the *seat roll technique* to get to the outside edge of the onside guard. Step with your back foot, then take a second step with your up foot and drive it into the center-guard gap. Drop your outside arm and leg and turn your body so that you are on your seat in an upright position getting ready to turn to the onside guard. As you are on the ground, get your head turned first to the outside of the guard so you can locate the ball while you're still on the ground. Just roll to the edge of the guard—not too far beyond him. You still want to try to control the gap. As you get to your feet, try to shuffle and make a play.

- As you attack the 1-gap, drive your far arm into the seam between the center and guard. You now can use the *spin technique*. After you drive into the 1-gap, take your inside arm (the arm nearest the ball) and drive it hard and low (into your opponent's hip area) trying to get around the guard's down block. At the same time, take your rear leg and drive it around trying to gain ground on the guard. Again, get your head turned around before your body so you can locate the ball.

- The fourth option is to use the counter spin technique. This technique should only be used if the offensive players are expecting either the seat roll or a spin technique. This technique is the same as the spin, only as you throw your near arm and leg, you should use the initial motion to fake the guard and now you simply come back around into the 1 gap without going all the way on the spin move.

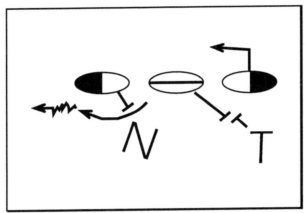

Diagram 4-5

- If the center drives down to the 3T without making contact, your reactions are now somewhat different. As you read your visual key, take your first step to the center. As you feel the onside guard (pressure key), drive hard and low straight upfield at heel depth of the guard; be ready to react to the football.

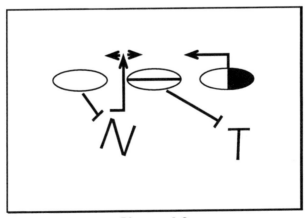

Diagram 4-6

5. Guard Pulls Away From You

You are now on the backside of the play. Refer to any previous discussion of a backside block for directions regarding how to read and react.

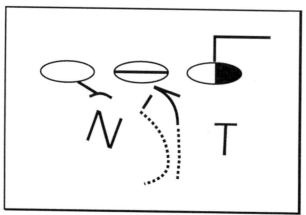

Diagram 4-7

6. Guard Steps Down One Step and Turns Away From You

This action is a *fan block* which indicates you are on the frontside of the play. This situation is usually an isolation play in which you will be double-teamed by the center and the guard. You should treat this situation the same as if the guard pulls to you. Refer to block #4 for how to respond to a play in which a guard pulls to you.

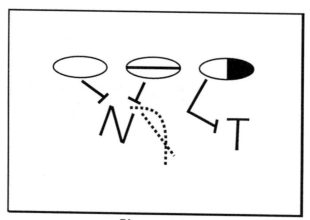

Diagram 4-8

7. Down Block

   Your visual key drives hard to the linebacker on your side. You are on the backside of a play. The center will more than likely base block you. As a result, you should attack the center as you would on any backside block. Maintain your gap and use the same rules as you would on any backside block. Attack the center and maintain your gap.

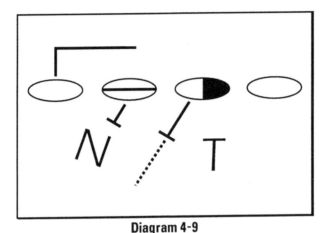

Diagram 4-9

8. Pass Set Block

   Your visual key will take a short step back. This action will indicate a draw or a pass play. Step with your back foot and attack the center with both hands. If you feel your pressure key working to you, anticipate a draw and drive up field without taking a side. Try to control the center and the onside guard so that neither one can come off on the linebacker. The key to a draw is a high double team trying to block you down the field. If they work on the line or back it will be a pass.

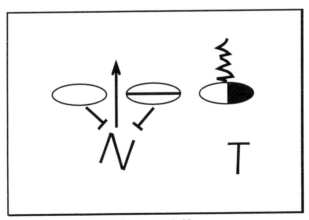

Diagram 4-10

1. Drop-Back Pass

   If the guard sets up for a drop-back pass, the noseguard should immediately locate his rush responsibility (1 gap) in the base defense. He should get his hands on the center quickly and execute his pass rush techniques. He should recognize whether he is being doubled or not. Turn your body (always facing the QB)—you must get at least three yards for your move to be successful.

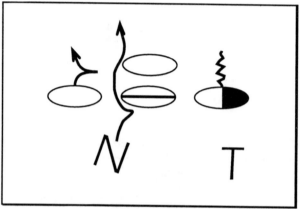

Diagram 4-11

2. Turn Back Protection

(The far guard will pass set). Play action (sprint draw) pass. If the center punches off on the noseguard and turns, the noseguard should be ready for the guard to pick him up. The noseguard should work the 1 gap, and fight his way up the field (Diagram 4-12A). If the center punches to him and the action is away, the noseguard should work either way on the center (Diagram 4-12B). You must determine where the QB will set-up on this protection.

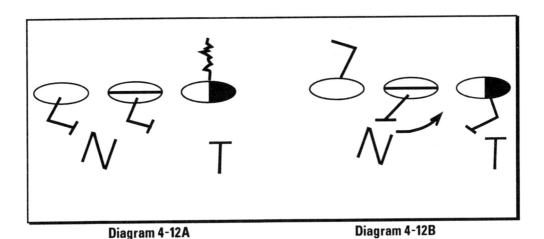

Diagram 4-12A   **Diagram 4-12B**

3. Slide Protection

(Full sprint). If the far guard steps inside and back, the noseguard should work across the face to the onside guard. The noseguard should find the quickest way to the quarterback. The QB in this situation will sprint out to the perimeter.

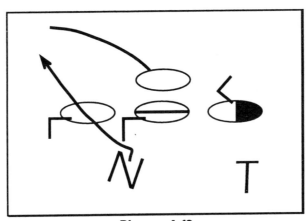

Diagram 4-13

3 Technique

- *Alignment*

    Align his inside eye on the outside eye of the offensive guard—two feet off the front tip of the football.

- *Stance*

    Assume a 4-point stance. Toe to instep relationship. His inside foot is back.

- *Key*

    The visual key is the onside guard. The pressure key is the onside tackle. Overall, the 3 technique should try to key the triangle—center/guard/tackle.

- *Responsibility*

    Run to: 3 gap to head up the offensive tackle. *Run away:* Squeeze and fight across the offensive guard's face. The 3 technique should squeeze the 1 gap. *Pass rush:* through the outside shoulder of the onside guard.

- *Movement and blow*

    Move on the movement of the onside guard. The 3 technique should watch the onside guard's headgear, step with the inside foot and try to get three steps north. As he steps, the 3 technique should try to place both hands on the chest of the blocker and strike a blow. The L.O.S. must be pressed.

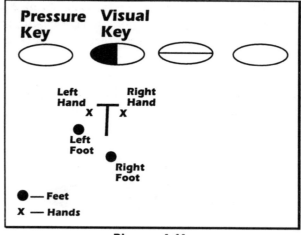

Diagram 4-14

1. Base Block
   Step with the inside foot. The 3 technique should strike a blow with both of his hands to the chest of the onside guard. The 3 technique should control the L.O.S., while keeping his outside arm free. All contact should be just off the mid-line of the visual key.

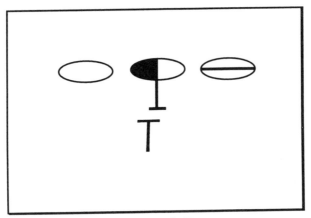

Diagram 4-15

2. Reach Block
   Step with the inside foot. As the 3 technique reads the head gear of the onside guard reaching him, the 3 technique should widen with him and press upfield, while keeping his shoulders square. As the 3 technique presses, he should lock his arms out to gain separation. The 3 technique should slide his far arm to the shoulder that is turning to him. This action will square his shoulders. A key coaching point on any reach block is to move your hips to gain control of your gap. Most players concentrate too much on using their the upper body and not keeping their hips down.

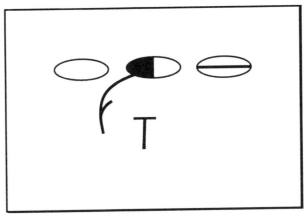

Diagram 4-16

3. Double Team

Step with the inside foot. The 3 technique should defeat the onside guard's block first. Maintain the L.O.S. As the 3 technique feels his pressure key, he should step hard into the onside tackle. If the 3 technique can drive his far arm through the seam between the onside guard and the onside tackle, he can split the double team. If not, he should throw his far arm to the ground and drop to his far knee. He should then execute a seat roll and attempt to build a pile. He must make sure that he "uses up" both the offensive guard and the offensive tackle.

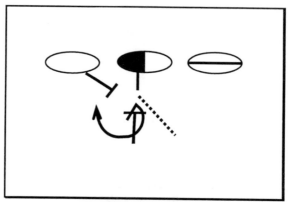

Diagram 4-17

4. Guard Pulls Frontside

As the 3 technique reads the drop step of the onside guard, he should expect a down block from the onside tackle. The 3 technique should maintain an inside relationship on the onside tackle. After he has taken his first step, he should attack the onside tackle with his outside foot and hip and drive the L.O.S. As soon as possible, the ball should be located. When there is not a cutback threat to the 3 gap, the 3 technique should pull with his outside arm and rip under the tackle. The 3 technique should then accelerate and get to the ball.

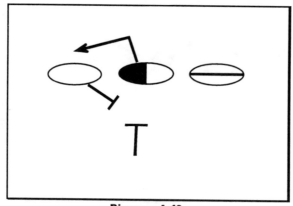

Diagram 4-18

5. Guard Pulls Farside

As the 3 technique reads the onside guard pulling to the farside, he should get himself as flat as he can to the L.O.S. and read the block of the center. In this situation, the center will be blocking back on the 3 technique. Accordingly, the 3 technique should be ready to strike a blow on the center. He should press the L.O.S. and only cross the face when there is no threat of a cut back.

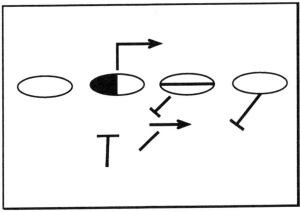

Diagram 4-19

6. Influence Trap

If the onside guard pass sets and then blocks out, it could be an influence trap. If the 3 technique doesn't feel pressure, he should turn his shoulders and close hard for the trap. The 3 technique should then take on the pulling guard with his outside shoulder, thereby forcing the ball to bounce. If a team uses both the influence trap and the sweep with the onside tackle blocking down, the 3 technique must respect the influence trap first by looking inside.

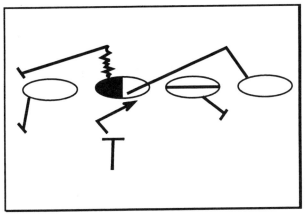

Diagram 4-20

7. Scoop Block

If the onside guard releases to the 3 technique's inside, the 3 technique should step with his inside foot and close with him. He should then squeeze the onside guard through the 1 gap, disrupting his course to the linebacker. All the while, the 3 technique should keep his shoulders square, and press the L.O.S.

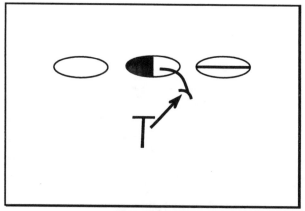

Diagram 4-21

8. Combo Block

If the onside guard comes out high to block the 3 technique on the 3 technique's inside breast plate, he should be aware of the combination block on the linebacker. This block is a tough read (it looks and feels like a double team). The onside guard, however, will come off of the 3 technique and the onside tackle will try to reach him. The 3 technique should squeeze the onside guard to the 1 gap and play the onside guard just like the scoop block. The 3 technique should make sure that the onside tackle does not get a reach block on him. The L.O.S. must be maintained. That response is the key to reacting effectively to a combo block.

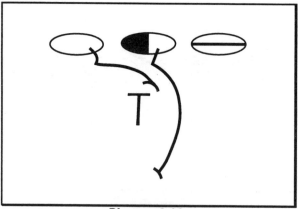

Diagram 4-22

9. Run-Through Block

If the onside guard takes a directional course to the linebacker, the 3 technique should get his hands on him and look for the onside guard trap/ trap option. If the 3 technique feels pressure from the onside tackle, he should get up the field two steps (counter play) and be ready to disrupt the pull of the guard or tackle.

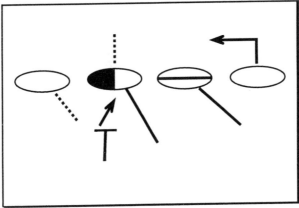

Diagram 4-23

10. Short Set

If the onside guard sets quick with no depth, the 3 technique should be ready for a draw. In this situation, the onside guard usually invites the 3 technique to the outside. The 3 technique should attack the onside guard and retrace his steps. The 3 technique is the key because he will get single-blocked on a draw play.

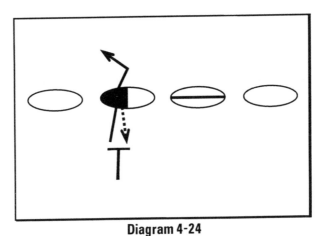

Diagram 4-24

1. Drop-Back Pass

   If the onside guard sets up for a drop-back pass, the 3 technique should locate his pass rush land marks. The 3 technique should get his hands on the blocker and execute his pass rush techniques. The 3 technique should rush through the gap in which he is aligned. He is the key to any pass rush because he can get widened almost on his initial move.

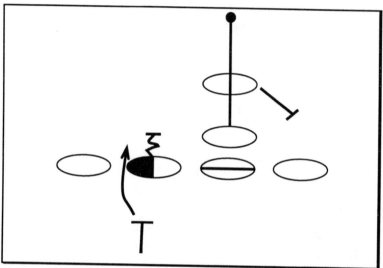

Diagram 4-25

2. Turnback Protection

   If the onside guard punches the 3 technique's breast plate and turns inside, the 3 technique should be ready to get picked up by the onside tackle. He should then work through the 3 gap and get up the field. He must know where the quarterback will set up on this protection scheme.

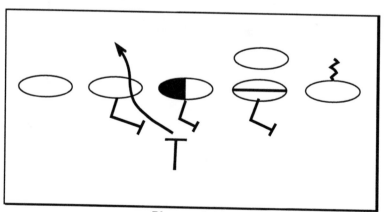

Diagram 4-26

3. Slide Protection #1

(Full sprint to the 3 technique). If the onside guard slides to the 3 technique's outside and works on the L.O.S., the 3 technique should be ready to attack the onside tackle. The onside tackle is usually the player assigned to pick-up the 3 technique. If the quarterback is on the run, the 3 technique may work across the face of the onside tackle.

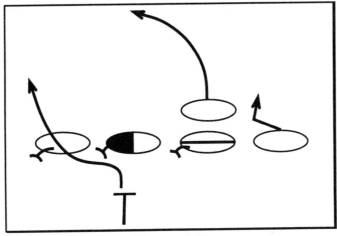

Diagram 4-27

4. Slide Protection #2

(Full sprint away from the 3 technique). If the onside guard sets up to the 3 technique's inside (off the L.O.S.), the sprint will be away from the 3 technique. The 3 technique should be ready to work to the center. The 3 technique may go across the center's face.

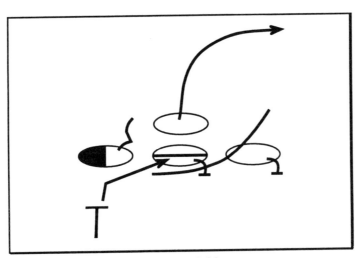

Diagram 4-28

5 TECHNIQUE
(His reactions are very similar to the 3T)

- *Alignment*
  Align his inside eye on the outside eye of the offensive tackle—two feet off the front tip of the football. If the 5 technique is on the hash mark, he may move to a head-up position (game plan).

- *Stance*
  Assume a 4-point stance. Toe-to-instep relationship. The 5 technique's inside foot is back.

- *Key*
  The visual key is the onside tackle. The pressure key is the tight end. Overall, the 5 technique should try to key the triangle of the onside guard/tackle/tight end. If the 5 technique has no tight end on his side of the ball, he does not have a pressure key. In that instance, the 5 technique should look for a running back that is cheated to the outside of the onside tackle. He should also look for a slot.

- *Responsibility*
  Run to: 5 gap to head up the tight end. Run away: Squeeze and release to the 3 gap. Pass: Contain on all passes unless the 5 technique is involved on a stunt to the inside.

- *Movement and Blow*
  The 5 technique should move on movement by the onside tackle. The 5 technique should watch the onside tackle's headgear. The 5 technique should then step with his inside foot and try to get three steps north. As he steps, he should try to place both hands on the chest of the onside tackle and strike a blow to the blocker's chest.

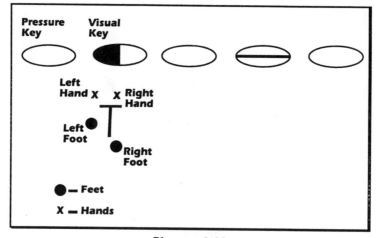

Diagram 4-29

1. Base Block
   Step with the inside foot. The 5 technique should strike a blow with both hands to the chest of the onside tackle. The 5 technique should control the L.O.S., keeping his outside arm free. Press the L.O.S.

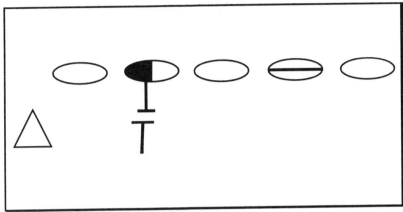

Diagram 4-30

2. Reach Block
   Step with the inside foot. As the 5 technique reads the headgear of the onside tackle reaching for him, he should widen with him and press upfield (keeping his shoulders square). As the 5 technique presses, he should lock his arms out to gain separation. The 5 technique should slide his far arm to the shoulder of the blocker that is turned to him. This action will square the 5 technique's shoulders. If his head gets caught inside, he shouldn't panic. As long as the 5 technique is pressing the L.O.S. and maintaining his position, he should keep working from his hips down. You must move your lower body.

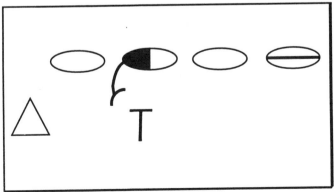

Diagram 4-31

3. Double Team

Step with the inside foot. The 5 technique should defeat the onside tackle's block first. The 5 technique should maintain the L.O.S. as he feels his pressure key. The 5 technique should step hard into the tight end. If he can drive his far arm through the seam between the onside tackle and the tight end, the 5 technique will split the double team. If not, the 5 technique should throw his far arm to the ground, drop his far knee to the ground, and seat roll.

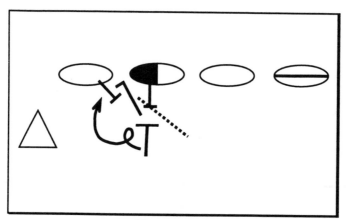

Diagram 4-32

4. Tackle Releases Inside

Step with the inside foot. The 5 technique should get his hands on the onside tackle to keep him off the linebacker. The 5 technique should stay square and look to the inside. The 5 technique should not close more than two steps.

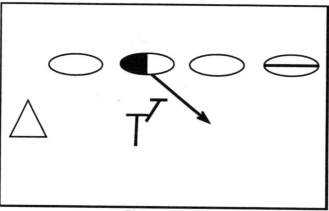

Diagram 4-33

- If it is a trap, the 5 technique should close to the ball laterally and drive through the trapper's inside so the ball has to bounce outside (i.e., trap the trapper). Make sure you attack the trapper just off the mid-line of the pulling guard.

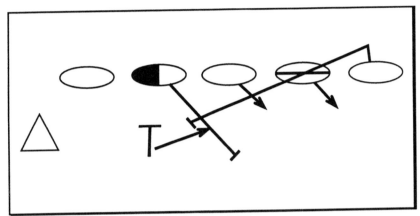

Diagram 4-34

- If it is an outside running play, the 5 technique should look to the running back on his side for a chop block. If the running back does not block, the 5 technique should locate the backside guard and the ballcarrier (watch for the trap option).

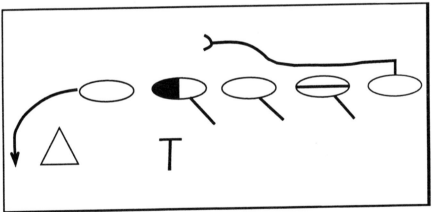

Diagram 4-35

- If it is a block from the near running back, the 5 technique should take him on with his outside shoulder, thereby using the blocker up and forcing the ball to bounce to the outside.

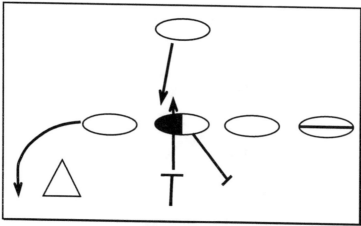

Diagram 4-36

- If it is a down block from the tight end, the 5 technique should close with the onside tackle as he veer releases inside. In the process, the 5 technique should deliver a hand shiver to disrupt the outside tackle's course. Then, as the 5 technique feels the tight end (pressure key) blocking down on him, he should explode upfield. If the 5 technique has penetrated the L.O.S., he should work behind the tight end's block. He can also spin to the outside if he is too late reacting to the tight end's block.

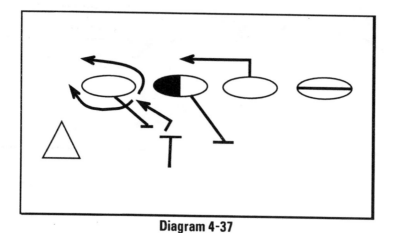

Diagram 4-37

5. Gut Block

If the onside tackle pulls inside and the onside guard blocks out on the 5 technique, the 5 technique should stay square and drive into the guard with his hands. If the ball commits inside, the 5 technique should work across the guard's face. As a general rule, this type of block isn't used much versus a 5 technique (much more so with a 4 technique).

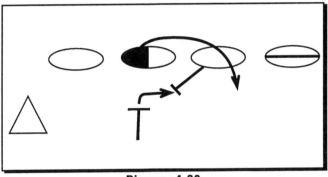

Diagram 4-38

6. Influence Trap

If the onside tackle pass sets and then blocks out, it could be an influence trap. The 5 technique should look inside and take on the trapper (i.e., trap the trapper). He should take him on with his outside (or upfield) arm. This is one time where he can turn his body and attack the trapper.

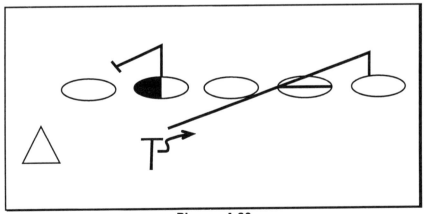

Diagram 4-39

7. "T" Block

If the onside tackle pulls out, the 5 technique should stay square and expect the tight end to block down on him. The 5 technique should get his hands underneath and work to the tight end's face to the outside, only after there is no threat that the ball will cut back.

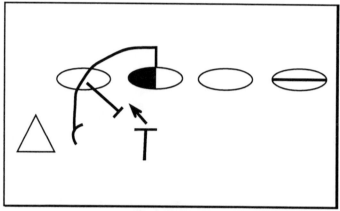

Diagram 4-40

8. Counter Boot

When the onside tackle pulls, the 5 technique should widen his base and work upfield to the depth of the quarterback. The 5 technique should expect the boot pass. He should always keep his head upfield while forcing the quarterback to stay inside him. If the ball is handed off and going away from him, the 5 technique should flatten to the ball. He must always be to the outside of any possible blocker. Remeber the rule: "Tackle pull away— stay, bootleg your way."

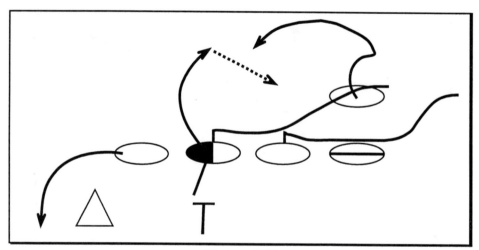

Diagram 4-41

9. High Wall (Backside Block)
   When the onside tackle steps inside and invites the 5 technique outside, the 5 technique should attack the inside shoulder of the onside tackle and press the L.O.S. The 5 technique should keep his shoulders square to him, maintain his gap, and remember that he also has to make a play inside of him.

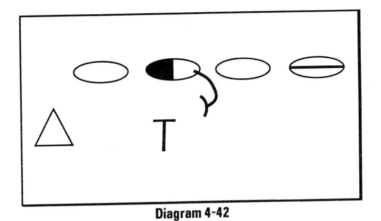

Diagram 4-42

Pass Reads

1. Drop-Back Pass
   If the onside tackle sets up for a drop-back pass, the 5 technique should immediately locate his pass rush landmarks. The 5 technique should get his hands on the onside tackle and execute his pass rush techniques. All pass rushes must start on the outside shoulder of the offensive lineman. Contact with lineman must be made by the 5 technique's third step. If the 5 technique gets a "me" call from the drop, he should take the inside pass rush.

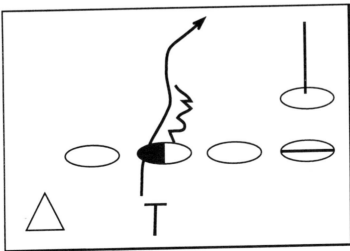

Diagram 4-43

2. Turn Back Protection

- If the onside tackle fires out and works on the line, the 5 technique should be ready for a play action pass. The 5 technique should work to his outside and keep contain.

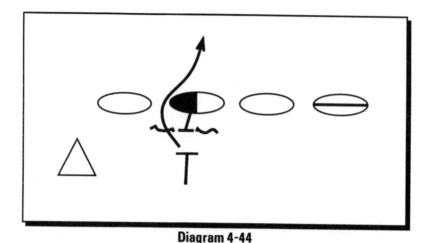

Diagram 4-44

- If the onside tackle hinges back and to the inside, the 5 technique can treat it like a sprint pass away. The 5 technique should remember, however, that he is still responsible for CRC (counter, reverse, cutback). It is critical that he sees the quarterback's jersey numbers and rushes behind the L.O.S. In all likelihood, the quarterback should be pulled up. He must be ready for the quarterback to scramble.

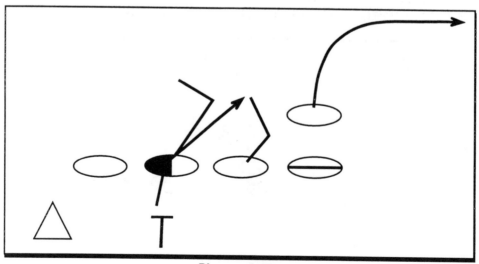

Diagram 4-45

3. Sprint Pass #1

(Toward the 5 technique). The 5 technique should immediately use his hands, and fight through the blocker. The 5 technique should drive laterally upfield, while always keeping the quarterback in front of him. The important point to remember is that the 5 technique should stay on his feet.

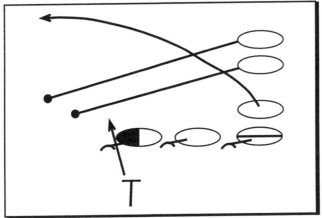

Diagram 4-46

4. Sprint Pass #2

(Away from the 5 technique). The 5 technique should react to the block. He has contain responsibility. Even though he is on an all-out rush, if the quarterback turns back, the 5 technique must come under control and force him deep. If the quarterback pulls up and looks through his lane, the 5 technique should get his hands up. The 5 technique should always keep his head upfield on the quarterback, while not allowing him to reverse his field and beat him over the top.

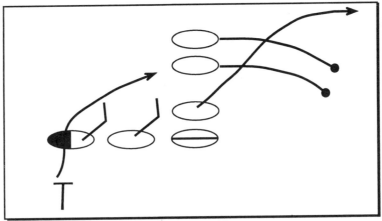

Diagram 4-47

RIP/SKIN TECHNIQUES

Along with playing our lineman in a normal reading technique, we also employ two other techniques that are essential in giving our lineman a three-way go.

The first technique is called a "Rip" technique. This tells any of our down-lineman that they are going across the face of the player that are aligned on. For example, the 5 technique tackle aligns as normal over his offensive tackle. A particular defense tells him to employ a rip technique.

Anytime we use this particular technique, the 5T assumes his normal stance and alignment. His weight should be on his up foot. Our linemen key the football anytime they are involved in a line stunt. As the ball is snapped, his first step is up and at a 45-degree angle to his visual key (in this case the offensive guard). As he steps, he will rip his backside arm (the arm away from the football) and dip the same shoulder. He is trying to avoid the tackles block and avoid contact with him.

As you step, you are reading your visual key. If he comes to you—plant on your first step and redirect with your second step. Stay on the outside edge of the guard. The ball is coming back to you.

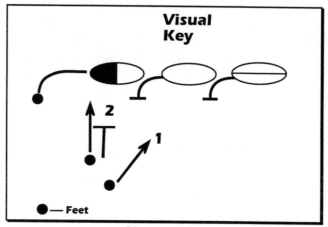

Diagram 4-48

If he goes away from you—keep going down the line as fast as you can because the ball is going away from you. You must step and shuffle without crossing over.

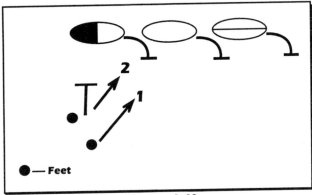

Diagram 4-49

The second technique is called a "Skin" technique. This tells any of our down lineman that they are going to the outside of the player that they are aligned on. For example, the 3 Technique tackle aligns as normal over his offensive guard. A particular defense tells him to employ a Skin Technique.

Anytime we use this particular technique, the 3T assumes his normal stance and alignment. His weight should now be on his back foot so he can push off and take his first step with his up foot. This step should be up and out. His visual key is now shifted to the offensive tackle. He now reads his key and reacts accordingly.

If the tackle (visual key) blocks down, you should go across his face and flatten down the line. You are on the frontside of the play usually a sweep.

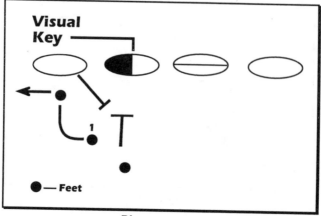

Diagram 4-50

If the tackle comes flat to you, take your first step up and out. Your second step should go straight as you fit between the offensive tackle and the offensive guard because you are on the backside of a play. Flatten down the L.O.S. Get to the hip of the offensive guard.

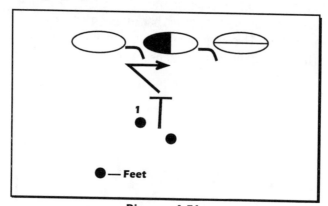

Diagram 4-51

In both techniques it is essential to practice with a right- and left-handed stance making sure you work on both a frontside and backside read. In chapter five when we build our stunts, you will see how we incorporate the rip and the skin techniques into our various defenses.

DRILLS FOR SHEDDING BLOCKERS

Drill 4-1: Base, Reach, Down

Objective: To teach the nose, the 3T, and the 5T to read their visual keys and to react to the three basic blocks.

Equipment needed: Nerf football

Description: The drill involves a nose guard (always working against two guards and a center) a 3T, and a 5T with their visual keys lined up across from them. Begin with all defensive players in a right-hand stance. The first block used in the drill is a base block. All three groups go at the same time. After each play, the next player in line moves up and the defensive man becomes the offensive man. The offensive man moves to the back of the line. When he gets to the front of the line, the drill is repeated using a left-hand stance. Then proceed to the reach block (both stances) and then the down block (both stances). Again because defensive players flip sides, defenders must use both stances.

Coaching points:
- Check for proper stance, alignment, and first steps.
- Always have the next player in line helping the player in front of him, because a coach can't see all three groups working.
- Make sure on contact that all players are in a proper football position and maintain their leverage.
- Ensure that defenders try to take as many steps north as possible.
- Require that defenders lock out—then shuffle a couple steps to the block.

T	G	GCG
5T	3T	N
5T	3T	N
5T	3T	N

Diagram 4-52

Drill 4-2: Read and React

Objective: To teach the nose guard, the 3T, the 5T to read their visual keys and to react to a specific blocking scheme; to give defenders the opportunity to work against combination blocks.

Equipment Needed: None

Description: The drill involves several players, including three on defense (a nose guard, a 3T and a 5T). On offense, the NG will have two guards and a center. The 3T will have a guard and a tackle. The 5T will have a tackle and a tightend. The drill begins with the 5T. The coach starts the drill by showing the offensive T and TE with a hand movement the particular blocking scheme he wants them to employ. The 5T defeats the block. The coach then rotates the 5T to the TE spot and the TE to the T and the T to the back of the line. Players rotate clockwise. The coach then moves to the 3T with a scheme. It could be the same scheme or a different one. After the 3T is finished, the coach moves to the NG with a particular scheme. Once the defender has correctly defeated the scheme, the drill is over.

Coaching Points:
- The emphasis should be placed on stance, alignment and first steps.
- The coach should make sure that he employs front-side as well as back-side schemes.
- The coach should make sure each defender uses both a right and left hand stance.
- This drill should be done at a teaching tempo.

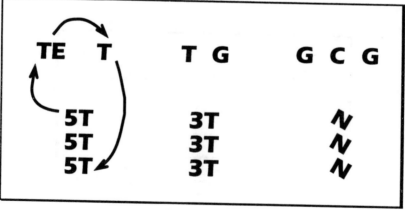

Diagram 4-53

Drill 4-3: Two-Man Shiver

Objective: To develop and practice the techniques involved in performing a hand shiver; to teach the skills to ward off a block; to improve reaction time.

Equipment needed: None.

Description: The drill involves four players: two blockers (B) and two defenders (D) (defensive linemen). Having given the blockers the snap count, the coach stands behind the blockers, facing the defenders. Responding to the coach's verbal count, the blockers fire out at the defenders. The defenders execute a hand shiver, control the blockers, and react to a hand signal given by the coach pointing out whether they should execute a left, right, or pass rush.

Coaching points:
- The proper techniques for striking a blow to a blocker should be emphasized—the heels of the hands should be driven forward and upward under the blocker's shoulder pads in an effort to straighten him up and neutralize his charge, the defender's elbows and wrists should be locked, and the defender should take short choppy steps until he determines his direction of pursuit.
- The drill can be performed with a two-man sled (in lieu of the two blockers).

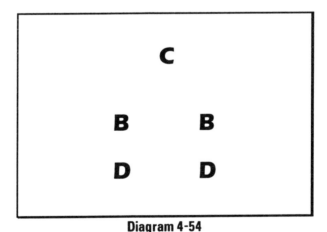

Diagram 4-54

CHAPTER 5

Building Defensive Fronts and Stunts

Why Use Different Fronts

Using different fronts and stunts is one of the most effective tools that a defensive coach has at his disposal. Before installing them into his defensive scheme, however, a coach should consider several points, including:

- *How much additional teaching is involved?*
  Football is a relatively simple, straightforward game, but it can be made too complicated for players by presenting too many ideas and techniques.

- *Everything starts with the base front (hawk defense).*
  All change-ups should be based on how they differ from the base defense.

- *Some different fronts are necessary.*
  If the same look is always given to an opponent, eventually that team will probably figure out a way to handle it. The point to remember is that a time and place exists when different looks are needed, without interfering with a team's base defense and without an excessive amount of teaching.

- *Certain fronts serve different purposes.*
  Keep in mind that certain fronts exist that will enhance a team's pass rush, as well as other fronts that can help in run defense. Accordingly, deciding which front to use in a particular situation usually depends on the specific situation. One of the primary jobs of a coach is to fit those pieces together without unduly interfering with his team's base defensive thoughts and philosophy.

- *Certain fronts allow for use of different personnel (nickel back, dime back).*
  To some degree, a team can give additional players the opportunity to participate. All factors considered, the greater number of players who actually get to play, the higher the potential positive impact on team spirit and morale.

- *Certain fronts are particularly suited to use against special offenses (the run and shoot, etc).*
  Sometimes particular defensive adjustments need to be made when playing against a special offense. Several specific fronts and stunts exist that can be employed to help defense unique offensive situations.

Building Zone Fronts and Stunts

When building different fronts and stunts, a coach should consider several factors, including:

- *Personnel vs. paper.*
  Put the right people in the right place to do the right thing. For example, although the safety blitz may look great on paper, the safety must be a player who is able to make the plays for the stunt to be consistently effective.

- *What are the strengths and weaknesses of each player?*
  Utilize players the best way possible. Play to their strengths. Have them do what they do best. Place them where they are needed. Most teams only have a few really outstanding players. The great players are going to play and do their thing anyway. It's coaching the rest of the relatively average players that can really make a difference.

- *All positions should be named.*
  Naming positions simplifies naming other fronts and stunts.

- *The role of each player in a particular stunt should be named.*
  For example, if the 5 technique has an inside move to make, it could be called "FIN". That moves a 5 technique inside. The important point to remember is that it doesn't have to be complicated. Above all, it should be made easy for the players.

- *The role of each player can be individualized or several actions can be grouped together and given a name.*
  For example, "SLANT" tells four players what to do. "LOOP" tells two players something. "FIN" tells one player. Offensive lines block pictures. The defensive coach's job is to distort the picture of the offensive line and make the offensive line hesitant. That should be one of the primary goals of the different fronts and stunts that are developed.

- *The choice of what stunts to use should be based at least in part on the scouting report.*
  Study what the offense likes to do and place personnel and build stunts accordingly. The goal of a coach is to create mismatches.

Hawk Defense

Hawk defense is the base defense. All the defensive personnel flip sides depending on one of six placement calls. The strong safety makes the call to determine which side the rush linebacker, the 3 technique, the eagle linebacker, the eagle corner, and the strong safety go. The nose, the inside linebacker, the 5 technique, the drop linebacker, and the drop corner go away from the call. The diagram below is a left placement.

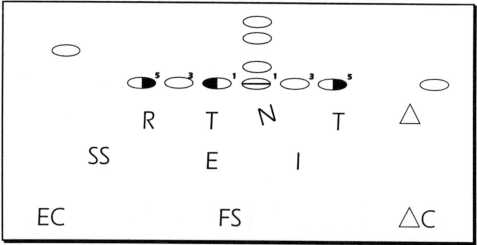

Diagram 5-1

R = rush linebacker   I   = inside linebacker
T = 3 technique   EC = eagle corner
N = tilted-nose   △C = drop corner
T = 5 technique   SS = strong safety
△ = drop linebacker   FS   = free safety
E = eagle linebacker

Numbers indicate gaps.
1 - Center - Guard gap on both sides.
3 - Guard - Tackle gaps on both sides.
5 - Tackle - TE gap on both sides.

We keep the same numbers on either side because we flip our people. A 3-Technique is only a 3T—and will align only over the guards.

Field (Tight, Strong) Hawk

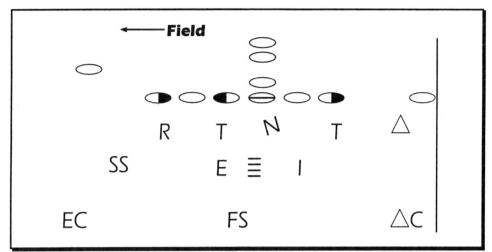

Diagram 5-2

Advantages: The reduction may be placed to the field, to the tight end, or to the strong side of the formation. Coverages may remain the same. We try to out number our opponents to the field, TE, our strength of the formation.

Short (Split, Weak) Hawk

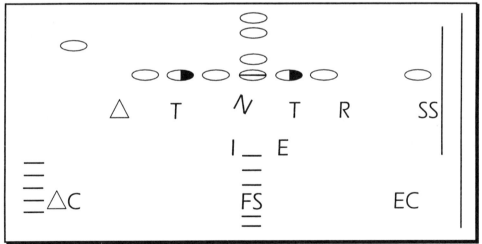

Diagram 5-3

Advantages: The reduction may be placed into the boundary, to the split end, or to the weak side of the formation. Coverages may remain the same.

STUNTS FROM THE HAWK DEFENSE

"Skin"
The nose guard "skins" into the 1 gap. His visual key remains constant.

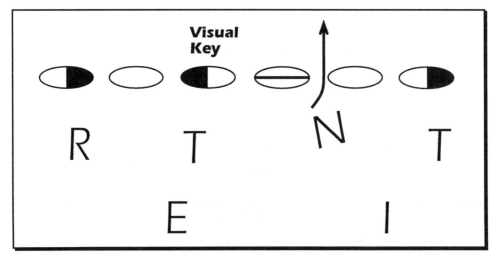

Diagram 5-4

"Shoot"
The eagle linebacker shoots the center-guard gap and the nose guard "skins."

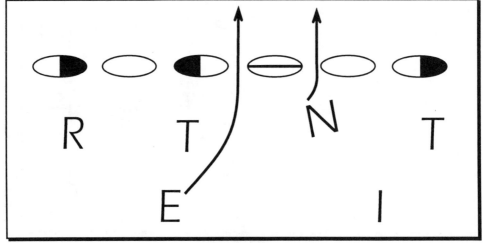

Diagram 5-5

"Loop"
The rush linebacker and 3 technique employ a 'skin' technique. Effective against a down block scheme on sweeps. Not as effective versus pass.

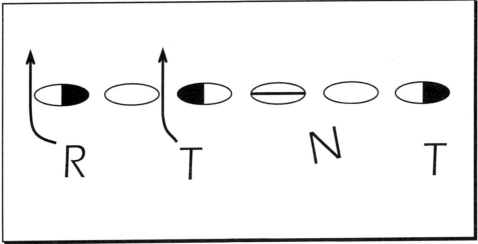

Diagram 5-6

"Fin"
The 5 technique uses a rip technique to get across the OT face. He reads the guard he is going to. The linebacker must scrape if the ball comes his side. Dotted line indicates what will happen on a pocket pass.

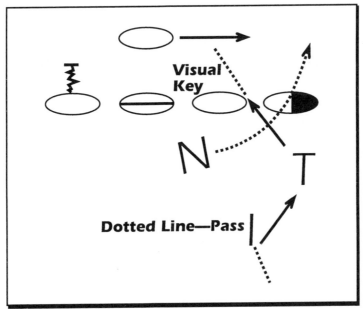

Diagram 5-7

"Gap"

The nose guard and the 3 technique get in a three-point stance and attack upfield through the outside neck of the center and the guard respectively. A good two-man pressure stunt against counterplays and play-action pass plays.

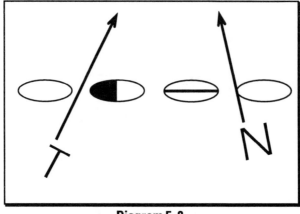

Diagram 5-8

"Slide"

The nose guard moves over into a 2 technique. Outside foot is now back and his visual key is now the 'C.' This front is not complicated. It, however, gives a defense an effective different look up front versus a strong tight end tendency team.

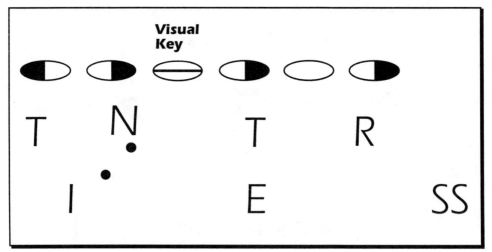

Diagram 5-9

"Falcon"

In this front, the 5 technique moves to a 4 technique. In a passing situation, the nose comes around to contain. This front is particularly effective against cut back plays.

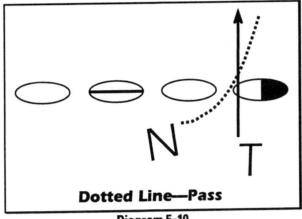

Dotted Line—Pass

Diagram 5-10

Split Tilt

The 3 technique kicks down to a 1 technique and tilts. Both the nose guard and the 3 technique cross key to the far guard. Both take a "skin" step and are 1 gap players.

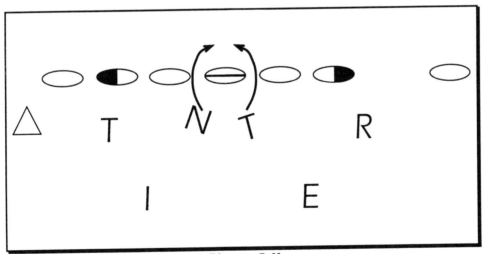

Diagram 5-11

"Cyclone"

The nose moves to a zero technique and the 5 technique moves to a 3 technique. The inside linebacker moves over the tackle. This front is used as a change up. This front gives the nose a two-way go in a pass situation.

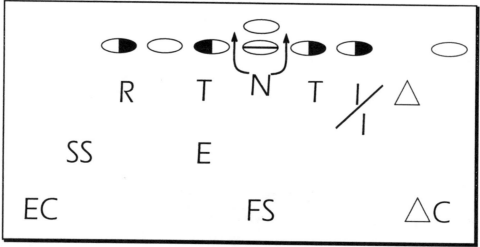

Diagram 5-12

30 Front

The 30 front is a four-man pass rush change up. This front will spring the rush backer many times when the tight end is going out on a pass play and allow him to be one-on-one with a RB.

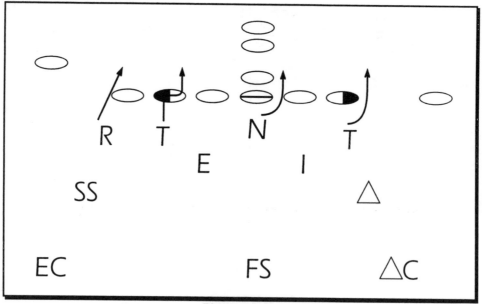

Diagram 5-13

40 Front

The 40 front is used in passing situations and is similar to the slide defense. A coach should try to play the upfront players head up so the offense doesn't know what gap they have.

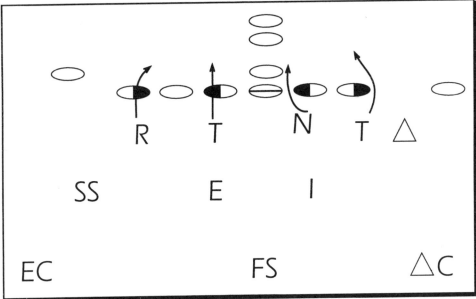

Diagram 5-14

STUNT FROM THE 40 FRONT

"Double Pick"

The nose and 3 technique attack the outside edge of their guard and swing their butt around to try to knock off the tackles—contain. The rush linebacker and the 5 technique drive upfield two steps then come under the inside rushers. This stunt is very effective versus teams that run the draw. Coaches' point: If you are an outside rusher—keep coming under—do not go back out!

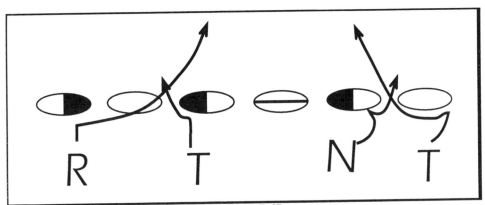

Diagram 5-15

CHAPTER 6

Tackling and Pursuit Fundamentals

Football is a game of contact. The true test of football (and often an action that involves relatively violent contact) is effective tackling. To a point, defensively, a team is no better than its ability to tackle properly. Proper tackling enhances the likelihood that a defensive team will achieve its three primary objectives—to gain possession of the football (i.e., to get the ball back for its offensive unit), to prevent an easy touchdown (i.e., to make its opponent earn every point it scores the hard way), and to score (i.e., to force the opponent's offense to give up a score to the defense).

On the other hand, poor tackling can prevent a defensive team from reaching its basic goals. Not only can a missed tackle allow an offensive team to retain possession of the ball, it may be the catalyst for either a long gain or an easy score. Poor tackling can also have a demoralizing effect on the defense and can diminish the effectiveness of the defense's own offensive team by effectively reducing the number of times the offense has the ball.

The Right Stuff

Effective tackling is a by-product of two basic factors—desire and technique. Of the two, most coaches believe that desire is the more important quality. As such, a defender should keep the following thought in mind at all times: "If I don't make the tackle, it can be a touchdown." A defensive player who has desire usually has a sufficient level of courage and determination to be able to tackle aggressively and effectively. Desire is a requisite trait for a defender who wants to punish the ball carrier. A defensive man who has the guts and desire to tackle aggressively can usually bring a ball carrier down regardless of the form he uses. Good form, however, enhances a defender's ability to tackle. Fortunately, proper tackling techniques can be taught.

Proper Tackling Techniques

All other factors considered, because the form for proper tackling can be taught, tackling ability can be improved. For a defensive player, the key is to understand the cardinal principles and fundamentals of effective tackling. We try to teach only three basic fundamentals in tackling:

1. Attack

   Whether the ball carrier is going east or west or coming at you, your first steps should be north (upfield to the ball carrier). You must close the seam—so the smaller the seam, the least amount of room to cut-back.

2. Chest to chest

   Chest-to-chest simply involves exploding your body with your numbers on the ball carrier's numbers. Your eyes should focus on the football. Any time contact is made, you should be in a football position, making sure all contact is made to the side of the football, while keeping your body between the head of the ball carrier and your shoulder on the side of the ball carrier carrying the football.

3. Dumpster

   Did you ever see the garbage trucks that have the arms that reach out to lift the big containers? That is how a defender's arms should lead; he should drive them up the sides of the ball carrier. Defenders should not drive their arms around the ball carrier. Many players have short arms and cannot come close to wrapping by trying to wrap around. This method allows anyone to control and make a tackle by drawing the arms up the side and then wrapping.

The key point to remember is to keep tackling simple—tackling is a "want to" skill!

TACKLING DRILLS

Drill 6-1: Form Tackling #1

Objective: To teach and practice proper form in tackling.

Equipment needed: None.

Description: The players spread out in lines facing the coach. On command from the coach, the players practice form tackling in a step-by-step manner. The tackler's knees should be bent. His hips should be lower than those of the ball carrier. His back should be straight with his head up. His eyes should be focused on the jersey number of the ball carrier. On contact, he should explode, rip up, and through the (simulated) ball carrier. Finally, he should drive his arms up the sides of the ball carrier.

Coaching points:
- This drill should be performed in just a walk-through fashion; it should never be performed live against a ball carrier. Make sure each defender practices tackling to each side (right and left).
- The relationship between using proper techniques while tackling and the safety of the tackler should be emphasized.

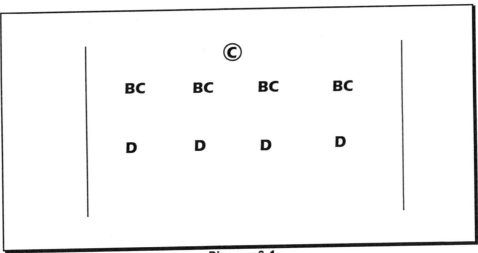

Diagram 6-1

Drill 6-2: Form Tackling #2

Objective: To teach and practice proper form in tackling; to enhance a defender's ability to visualize the proper defensive position.

Equipment needed: One football per line of players.

Description: The players line up in several lines facing the coach. The first player in each line acts as a ball carrier, while the next player serves as the tackler. On command from the coach, the ball carrier takes a position approximately one yard in front of the tackler, facing the tackler. The tackler assumes a "ready" position. On the next command from the coach, the ball carrier moves towards the tackler at about half speed. The tackler takes one step forward, dips his knees, makes contact on the jersey number of the ball carrier, and slides his eyes to one side. Driving up and through the ball carrier, the tackler then drives his arms up the side of the ball carrier.

Coaching points:
- This is a walk-through drill. Form should be emphasized.
- The ball carrier should run attacking the L.O.S. and the tackler to make it easier for the tackler to work on form.
- This drill is particularly useful early in the practice year.

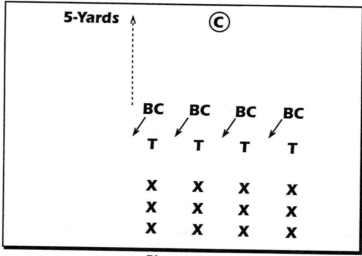

Diagram 6-2

Drill 6-3: Form Tackling #3

Objective: To teach and practice proper form in tackling.

Equipment needed: One football.

Description: The defenders are divided into two lines facing each other. One line is designated as tacklers, while the other line acts as ball carriers. On command from the coach, the ball carrier runs at about three-quarter speed to the tackler's right side. At a controlled speed, the tackler makes an angle tackle on the ball carrier. The ball carrier then rotates to the end of the tackler's line and the tackler to the ball carrier's line, respectively. After each tackler has practiced tackling to his right side, the ball carriers run to the tackler's left side. Each defender then makes a tackle to his left side.

Coaching points:
- The coach should position himself behind the ball carrier in order to observe the tackling techniques of the defender.
- The tackler should keep his head up, his eyes open and focused on the jersey number of the ball carrier, put his head across the front of the ball carrier, and drive his arms up the sides of the ball carrier.
- The coach should make sure players are not stopping on contact with the ball carrier.
- Make sure that the tackler doesn't false step. Body weight should be foward.

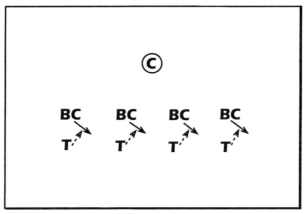

Diagram 6-3

Drill 6-4: Form Tackling #4

Objective: To teach and practice proper form in tackling; to develop explosiveness in tackling.

Equipment needed: A (one-man) sled.

Description: This drill involves teaching tackling in a step-by-step, progressive fashion. The players line up in front of the sled. On command from the coach, the drill begins by having the defender assume a proper contact position (for tackling) against the sled. This position is the one he should be in when initially making contact with a ball carrier. From this initial contact position, the defender next drives through the sled, driving his arms up on the sides of the sled, keeping his head up and his feet moving. He keeps driving through the sled until the coach blows the whistle. Finally, starting from a good hitting position approximately three yards from the sled, the defender fires into the sled at full speed, makes a proper tackle, and follows through until the coach stops play.

Coaching points:
- The relationship between form and safety should be emphasized.
- Proper body position and proper tackling techniques should be required during all steps of the drill.
- The coach make sure that every defender practices tackling using both shoulders (first one and then the other).
- After the proper technique is mastered you can roll a ball so that he can come off the machine and recover a fumble.

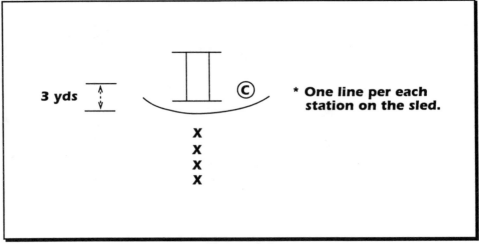

Diagram 6-4

Drill 6-5: Angle Tackling

Objective: To teach defenders to tackle properly after sprinting toward a ball carrier; to practice maintaining body control prior to tackling after running hard.

Equipment needed: A football (optional).

Description: The drill involves two players—each approximately two and a half yards away from a yard-line. One acts as a ball carrier, while the other serves as a tackler. On command from the coach, the ball carrier and the tackler sprint toward each other. The ball carrier can go right or left but should not go over the line. The ball carrier cannot use head fakes or fancy movement. The ball carrier should not be taken down.

Coaching points:
- The tackler must maintain a good base and keep his feet moving prior to making the tackle. Good breakdown position—make sure the tackler is moving his feet in place.
- Proper form and tackling techniques should be emphasized.
- The tackler should try to keep the ball carrier from gaining ground.

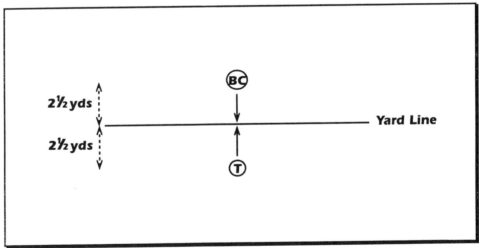

Diagram 6-5

Drill 6-6: Fillin' the Alley

Objective: To teach defenders to remain slightly behind a ball carrier when he is moving laterally; to teach defenders to attack from an inside position when the ball carrier turns up field; to practice proper tackling techniques.

Equipment needed: Four blocking dummies (bags); a football. If possible, flat agile bags should be used. Dummies that roll should not be used.

Description: The four blocking dummies should be laid on the ground parallel to each other, about 3-4 yards apart. The drill involves two players—one acting as a ball carrier and one as a tackler. The ball carrier should assume a position on the inside of the bag while the tackler starts on the outside of the bag. So that the tackler will be in an inside-out position on the football. On command from the coach, the ball carrier runs parallel to the dummies and then cuts up between two of the dummies (as predetermined by the coach). The tackler pursues laterally, remains slightly behind the ball carrier, and makes the tackle after the ball carrier has turned up the alley.

Coaching points:
- The tackler should not cross his feet while pursuing laterally.
- Proper form and tackling techniques should be emphasized.
- The tackler should maintain an inside-out approach.

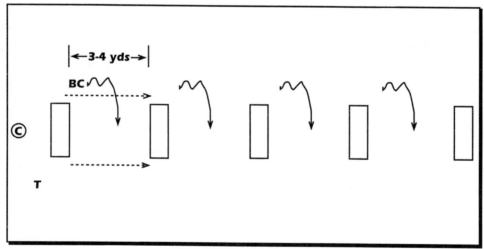

Diagram 6-6

Team Pursuit

One of the most important factors in defensive football is team pursuit. Team pursuit can be defined as a planned, coordinated system of converging on the ball carrier as quickly as possible, with each defender required to take proper angles of pursuit in order to achieve containment of the ball carrier within a desirable defensive perimeter. Hopefully, such containment will lead to several defenders arriving at the ball together, resulting in gang tackling. A coach cannot overly emphasize the importance and need for taking the proper angles of team pursuit and making gang tackles. Every defensive player should know his proper angle of pursuit and should be encouraged to hustle to tackle the ball carrier on every play.

TEAM PURSUIT DRILL

While a coach has the option of the many drills that exist to teach pursuit, this drill is one of the very best.

Drill 6-7: Team Pursuit

Objective: To teach defenders the principles and techniques of proper pursuit, using the correct angle and exerting maximum effort.

Equipment needed: A football; line spacing strip (optional); cones could be substituted instead.

Description: The ball is spotted on the 10-yard line either on either hashmark or in the middle of the field. All players are five yards deep in the end zone. On the coaches' command, the first group sprints to the football and forms a huddle. The coaches will give a defense with a coverage call. The players break the huddle and align in a formation which has coaches serving as a tightend and wide receivers. A coach or a backup quarterback will simulate a snap. On the snap, the defender will respond to the action— run, pass, draw or a quarterback scramble. Three coaches are placed around the field—a defensive back coach deeper than the deepest defender and two other coaches on the sideline, 10-20 yards downfield from the football. The head coach or the defensive coordinator stands behind the offense on the goal line.

- *Pass play:* The quarterback will drop back. The defensive line will rush. All other players will drop into coverage. The quarterback then throws the ball. All defenders sprint to the football. If the ball is intercepted, all players sprint through the goal line.

- *Run play:* The quarterback will fake a pitch either way. The defenders will take the proper angle to the coach on that particular sideline. All players will form around the coach, while keeping their feet chopping. If all is OK, the coach will give his signal of approval. At that point, all eleven defenders will do a quick up-down and sprint back to the huddle.

  As the players are coming back, either the head coach or the defensive coordinator will look to each of the three position coaches for a thumbs up. If any coach gives a thumbs down signal, the same group of defenders must repeat the drill and tell the players what mistake was made.

- You can also employ a draw or a QB scramble.

Coaching points:
- Proper huddle, break and alignment
- Proper angles to the football
- Intercept ball at its highest point
- Sprint to the coach or through the goal line

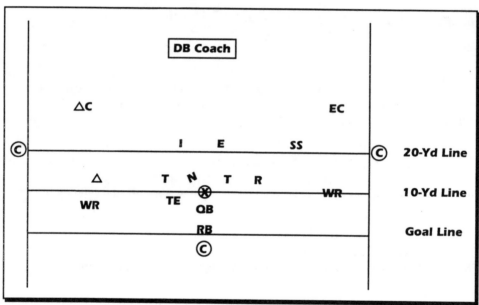

Diagram 6-7

CHAPTER 7

Pass Rush Fundamentals

Winning teams are able to combine a great pass rush with all of their defensive coverages. The basic key for a successful pass rush is to have an unrelenting desire to get to the passer. An effective pass rusher never lets up—he's always applying pressure. When the passer is being pressured (harassed, hit, sacked, etc.), it can become very difficult for him to concentrate on his receivers or the coverages he's facing.

One of the primary goals of a dominating defense is to shut down the rushing game of its opponent. When the rushing attack is stopped, a predictable passing situation is created. Once the threat of a run is virtually eliminated, a defensive team can take control of the game. Defenders are now thinking about factors that collectively will allow them to dominate the offense—sacking the quarterback, intercepting and returning a pass, hitting the quarterback while he is throwing the ball, breaking-up passes, etc.

Another major advantage of an effective pass rush is the effect it can have on the confidence levels of defenders assigned to man-to-man pass coverage. No one can dispute the fact that probably the most isolated place on a football field is the area where a defender is covering man-to-man. Not surprisingly, a good pass rush has a very positive impact on man-to-man coverage. A defense must be able to exert enough continuous pressure on the passer if the man-to-man defenders are to be able to cover closely and confidently. Otherwise, the quarterback may have too much time to throw, in which event, the coverage will often break down. Furthermore, each time the defensive line fails to harass the passer before he throws, the confidence level of a defender to closely cover his man man-to-man may be diminished.

Basic Pass Rush Fundamentals

The importance and necessity of adhering to certain pass rush fundamentals cannot be stressed enough. Among the factors that defensive linemen should understand and adopt are the following:

- Defensive linemen should key the football. They should anticipate and quickly recognize when a passing situation exists. Either by down and distance or reading offensive lineman stances or various formations.

- Defensive linemen should move quickly and decisively on their first step and should have a plan on what they're going to do depending upon how the offensive line reacts.

- A defensive lineman should contact the shoulder of his offensive opponent (lineman) by his third step.

- Defensive linemen should remember that an effective pass rush involves the coordinated action of their hands, feet, and head movement.

- A defensive lineman should keep his momentum toward the passer, without wasting any motion. Every step should be north. One of his primary objectives should be to get penetration into the quarterback's throwing lane and to force the passer to move from his packet and to divert the quarterback's attention.

- A defensive lineman should charge low when rushing the passer and keep his shoulders forward of his feet (i.e., body tilt) to prevent a blocker from getting under him.

- A defensive lineman should use the blocker's momentum.

- A defensive lineman should shed the blocker and burst by him before he can recover.

- A defensive lineman should keep his eyes focused on the quarterback while rushing the passer as his hands, feet, and eyes get him to the ball.

- A defensive lineman should stay in his lane when rushing the passer. If he is knocked out of his lane, he should work his way back into it.

- If a defensive lineman has not reached the quarterback and he starts to throw, the defender should get his hands up if the passer is facing him. If the quarterback is facing away from the defender, the defender should run through the passer from behind and should tackle him high and pin his arms to his sides. In this instance, if possible, the defender should attempt to knock the ball loose from the quarterback. Whenever you rush on the backside of the quarterback, think ball (you will get the sack).

- A defensive lineman who is serving as a contain man should keep his feet on the ground and should avoid being blocked beyond the quarterback.

- Defensive linemen should vary their rush techniques.

- Once a pass has been thrown, a defensive lineman should sprint and pursue in the direction that the ball was thrown to get in on a clean-up tackle, to help cause the receiver to fumble, or to help block if the pass is intercepted. Defensive linemen should be expected (required) to sprint at least five yards after the ball is thrown. If the pass is complete, the defender will already be sprinting toward the receiver.

Steps to Success

A defender who drives for the passer will...

- Squeeze the passer's area of operation.
- Force the passer out of his throwing area.
- Force the passer to run. (As a general rule most quarterbacks are not good runners.) Use your scouting report to chart the quarterbacks.
- Throw the quarterback for a loss.
- Cause the passer to fumble.
- Make the passer jittery as he moves away from the center—possibly causing him to throw the ball too quickly.
- Make the passer lose confidence in his protection.

A defender who gets his hands up will...

- Divert the quarterback's attention.
- Bat the ball—however, make sure you are going north.
- Tip the ball for an interception.
- Force a bad throw.
- Force the quarterback to pull the ball back and run.
- Force the passer to elevate his throw, which may give the secondary more time to adjust their range during coverage— perhaps resulting in an easy interception.

A defender who does not leave his feet prior to the release of the ball will...

- Limit the quarterback's opportunity for finding a new throwing lane.
- Maintain his balance.
- Maintain his ability to react and move quickly.
- Maintain his ability to adjust his movements (rush) as necessary.

Pass Rush Techniques

The various types of pass rushes can be grouped into two basic classifications — power rushes and speed rushes. Power rushes are "in-your-face", go-right-over-the-blocker defensive charges. Speed rushes, on the other hand, place the emphasis on having the pass rusher beat the blocker off the line of scrimmage. A description of the most commonly used power and speed rushes involves the following:

Power Rushes —mostly used by inside rushers.

- Bull rush: Designed to drive the blocker into the quarterback. The defender accelerates across the line of scrimmage and explodes, using leverage into half of the surface of the blocker. He drives his hands up through the armpits of the blocker. He should keep his feet moving and should be relentless in his charge.

- Swim technique: The defender accelerates across the line of scrimmage and using leverage explodes into half of the surface of the blocker. He drives his inside arm up through the chest plate of the blocker. He should grab cloth on the outside of the blocker's shoulder pad with his outside arm. He should do everything possible to convince the blocker that the defender is on a bull rush charge. When the blocker lunges or overextends forward, the defender should pull hard with his outside arm, while simultaneously crossing over and stepping beyond the blocker with his inside foot (i.e., "swims" over the blocker's surface with his inside arm). The defender's objective is to replace the blocker's body with his. The defender should then push off and accelerate to the quarterback. He should use a "punch through" technique over the shoulder, so that he doesn't expose the entire side of the body.

- Rip technique: Similar to the swim technique for pass rushing, the defender should accelerate across the line of scrimmage. The defender should convince the blocker that the defender is on a bull charge. Upon contact, rather than using a swimming technique, the defender should rip up through the blocker's surface with his inside arm. The defender then "reloads" to come free if necessary. The defender should remember to rip to the sky and lean into the blocker.

Speed Rushes

- Quick swim: This technique can also be used with a head fake. The defender should accelerate across the line of scrimmage. He should reach for the blocker's outside shoulder or forearm and grab and pull it, while executing a swim technique. If the blocker quickly locks his arms out, the defender should club at the blocker's elbow and execute the swim technique.

- Quick rip: 1 technique or 2 technique—The defender accelerates across the line of scrimmage, executes a rip technique into the gap, dips his arm, and continues to reload. He may spin back to the quarterback as he reaches his desired depth position. 3 technique or 5 technique—The defender accelerates across the line of scrimmage, grabs and pulls the blocker, and executes a rip technique. Using leverage, the defender engages the blocker's surface and rips up through the armpit (turning the blocker's shoulders). The 3 technique may spin back to the quarterback.

- Shoulder turn: The defender accelerates across the line of scrimmage and jams the blocker's outside shoulder pad hard. He continues to push on the shoulder pads until he is able to turn the blocker's shoulders, as the defender maneuvers the blocker's body to a position perpendicular to the quarterback. The defender then executes a rip technique to get beyond the blocker to get at the quarterback.

- Counter move off the shoulder turn: The defender accelerates across the line of scrimmage and jams the blocker's outside shoulder pad hard. The defender must convince the blocker that it is the defender's intention to go around him to get to the quarterback. As the blocker fights to regain his position and his head pops beyond the defender's head, the defender should throw the blocker aside with his inside arm. The defender then executes a rip technique under the blocker's surface to the inside.

- Counter move off the rip technique: The defender executes a quick rip upfield. As he nears or reaches the depth of the quarterback, the defender pivots off his inside foot, spinning underneath the blocker. The defender should club and clear the blocker using his outside arm. He then accelerates to the quarterback. It is important that the defender convinces the blocker that it is his intention to beat the blocker over the top. He should gain ground with his "swing" leg.

- The defender should also work on a speed rush move of his own. For example, a combination of several of the aforementioned moves offers a defender an excellent possible option.

PASS RUSH DRILLS

Drill 7-1: Lineman Takeoff

Objective: To teach a proper sprinter's stance to defenders with the hand nearest the football down; to practice reacting to ball movement.

Equipment needed: A football.

Description: The drill involves the coach and four players. Representing interior offensive linemen, the cones (or blocking dummies) are set up five yards apart on a yard line. Standing between the cones, a manager snaps the ball to the coach. On movement of the ball, the four defenders (D) sprint low and hard across the line of scrimmage and converge on the quarterback at six yards.

Coaching points:
- The coach should use various kinds of cadence before snapping the ball in order to get the defenders used to reacting to the ball, as opposed to the "quarterback's" voice inflections. A manager or an injured player can snap the ball.
- The coach should remind the defenders that their first priority is to key the football and sprint six yards.
- After each rep, the players should switch sides so they can attack from both sides, then flip sides.

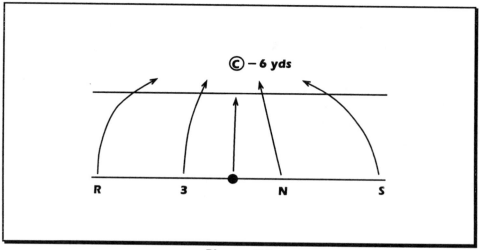

Diagram 7-1

Drill 7-2: Lineman Take-Off with Tennis Balls

Objective: To teach the proper sprinter's stance; to practice reacting to the snap of the football; to develop hand coordination and quickness.

Equipment: One (Nerf) football; two tennis balls; a firm surface.

Description: The drill involves two players, a coach, and someone to assimilate a snap. As the ball is snapped, the player's eyes focus on the tennis balls that are being held by the coach who is positioned three yards from the football. The coach has his arms out with his body forming a "T." Players react to the dropping of the tennis ball by the coach and try to catch the ball before it hits the ground a second time. After all players go a depth of three yards from the coach, the coach can move back to four yards, etc. A depth of five to six yards from the coach is considered particularly challenging. The coach should be particularly alert once the competitive level of the drill is increased and players start diving for the tennis balls.

Coaching points:
- Coach will drop the ball as the manager snaps the ball.
- Proper stance (inside hand down).
- Proper takeoff.
- Focus on the tennis ball after the snap.
- Catch the ball.
- Good pre-season drill—first or second day drill.

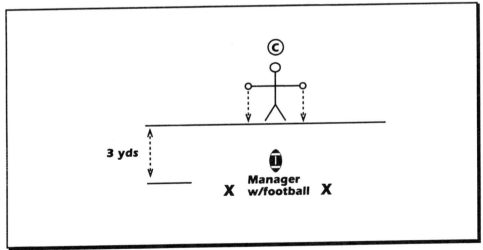

Diagram 7-2

Drill 7-3: Attack-Pass Rush

Objective: To teach and practice the basic fundamentals and techniques involved in a bull rush (power pass rush).

Equipment needed: None.

Description: The drill involves having the defenders split up into two lines facing each other approximately one yard apart. One line is designated as blockers (O), while the other line serves as pass rushers (D). On command from the coach, the defenders accelerate across the area in front of the players blocking them and explode into the blockers. Using leverage, each defender drives his hands up through the armpits of the blocker he is facing. Defending his "turf," the blocker attempts to prevent the defender from advancing. Contact continues for a predetermined time (e.g., 3-5 seconds) until the coach blows his whistle. After a set number of repetitions, the players switch roles. All players should bull rush the same direction so that collisions are avoided. Make sure there is ample distance between each group of players.

Coaching points:
- The drill should first be performed at a controlled speed and then subsequently at full speed once the basic movement mechanics have been mastered.
- The coach should emphasize the need for an explosive blow (strike) by the defender rather than a push.
- The first step by the defender should be with his inside foot.
- The coach can move around to get various angles.

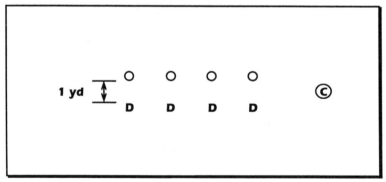

Diagram 7-3

Drill 7-4: Back Foot Carioca Drill

Objective: To teach a method to cut the edge on a pass rush.

Equipment needed: None.

Description: The drill involves having the players (D) pair up and position themselves so that each defender is aligned to the side of the offensive player. A defender's hands should be on the shoulder (grabbing cloth) of the offensive player. On the command of the coach, the defender should pull down on the shoulder and at the same time take his inside foot and use a Carioca move to get his hips beyond the blocker. The defender should then accelerate to the quarterback.

Coaching points:
- The defender should be in a leverage position to start the drill.
- The defender should pull down on the shoulder of the offensive player.
- All players should use their back foot (i.e., no false steps). In this case the right foot will carioca behind the left foot.
- The defender should accelerate to the quarterback.

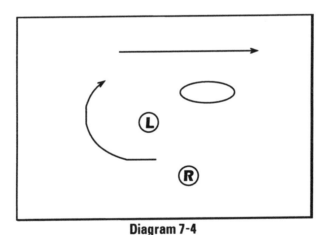

Diagram 7-4

Drill 7-5: Pass Rush Lanes

Objective: To develop the ability to stay in rush lanes.

Equipment needed: Football/lines painted on the field. You should leave at least
two areas so you can alternate the drill. Save the grass.

Description: Five offensive players and five defensive players aligned in their lanes.
One of the five defenders is designated as "live". On the cadence (used
by the offense), the "live" defender will execute a pass rush move and
attempt to drive to the quarterback. The quarterback is in a shotgun
position. A coach should move from left to right on defense to
determine who is "live." After a defender goes "live", he is replaced by
another defender.

Coaching points:
   · To teach lane responsibility and distance to quarterback.
   · A good "go" vs. the offense.
   · All five defenders key and move forward on the snap of the ball.
     However, one is live. This is predetermined as we go from left to right.

Things to remember about the pass rush:
   · All steps should go north.
   · Players should work in a right and left hand stance.
   · A standup dummy should never be used as a quarterback in this drill
     because offensive players can get knocked back into it, causing injury.
     A better option is to use a manager, etc.
   · No pushing should be allowed; a pass rush move should be used *every*
     time.
   · The focus should be to practice good repetitions every time.

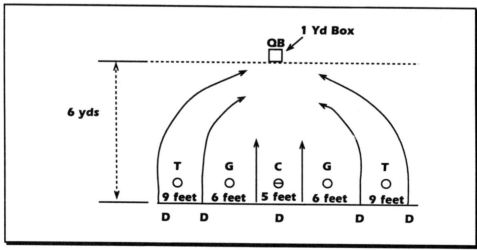

Diagram 7-5

Drill 7-6: Lock, Lift, and Spin

Objective: To develop the ability to use leverage; to practice the spin technique; to improve ability to shed the blocker.

Equipment needed: None.

Description: The drill involves dividing the defenders into two groups. One group acts as offensive blockers (O), while the other group serves as pass rushers (D). The drill begins by having the players pair up and line up facing opposite directions on a yard line, next to each other, hip to hip. On command from the coach (C), the defensive player dips his underarm and using leverage, explodes into the blocker in an attempt to dislodge him off of the yardage line. Simultaneously, the blocker uses his hands and his body in an attempt to prevent any movement by the defender across the yardage line. After a predetermined number of repetitions, the players switch roles.

Coaching points:
- The coach should emphasize the proper techniques for applying leverage.
- The drill continues at full speed until the coach blows his whistle. Each player should go full tilt until he hears the whistle.

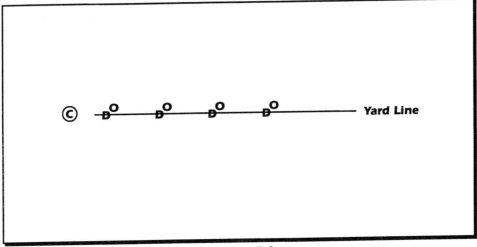

Diagram 7-6

CHAPTER 8

Movement Fundamentals

A strong argument can be advanced that a more realistic measure of football speed for a defensive player is how quickly a defender can react and move to the ball. Although foot speed can be an important factor in football, how fast a player can run 50-100 yards straight ahead is not directly related to quickness, reaction time, and agility. In fact, in many football situations, quickness, reaction time, and agility may play a more critical role for defensive players than foot speed. Fortunately, to a point, football players can develop these particular motor skills.

One of the most effective methods for developing movement (motor) skills is through the repetitive use of drills. The next section of this chapter presents several drills that have been designed to enhance agility and reaction time and to improve movement skills. By no means is the offering of drills inclusive. If necessary, coaches should redesign these drills (or add new ones) to fit their situation and the ability levels of their athletes.

AGILITY AND REACTION DRILLS

Note: All drills involve three men up front with no player going more than ten yards.

Drill 8-1: Quick Feet

Objective: To warm-up; to develop quick moving feet and lateral movement reaction while in a good movement position.

Equipment needed: None.

Description: The players spread out in three lines facing the coach. They assume a good football position— head erect, back flat, shoulders square, a slight bend at the knees and waist, their arms hanging loosely in front of their body, and their weight supported on the balls of their feet. On command from the coach (i.e., "ready"), each player starts moving his feet quickly in place. The coach then gives a directional signal (clenched fists together with his thumbs flashing the direction he wants the players to move laterally). After several change of directions laterally, the coach then gives a command (i.e., "ready, ready") that requires the players to reassume their starting position, quick moving feet, etc. After repeating the pattern several times, the coach raises his arms to signal to the players to sprint past him. Players can stay at the other end and repeat the drill by running the other direction. Player should yell pass when the coach raises his hands.

Coaching points:
- Emphasis should be placed on action-reaction, proper body position, proper body movement, and quickness.

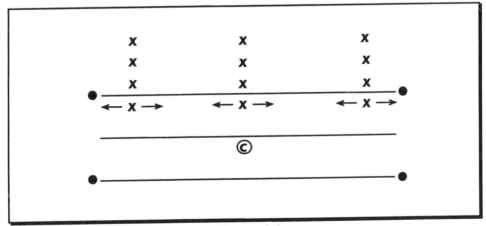

Diagram 8-1

Drill 8-2: Seat Roll

Objective: To warm-up; to develop the ability to quickly get off the ground in proper body position.

Equipment needed: None.

Description: The players spread out in three lines facing the coach. The players then assume a good movement position (refer to Drill 8-1 for a description). On command from the coach (i.e., "ready"), the players drop to the ground on all fours (hands and feet) with their feet chopping. The coach visually signals to the players whether they should roll left or right. After a set number of repetitions, the coach signals with his arms up in the air and the players sprint past him as they yell pass. Three or four movements are sufficient.

Coaching points:
- This drill is appropriate for all defensive players.
- The players should keep their heads up and their eyes focused on the coach even while rolling on their butts.
- The players' eyes should come around before their bodies do.
- You can do this drill from a two-point stance.
- Players should move up one yard in front of the cones.

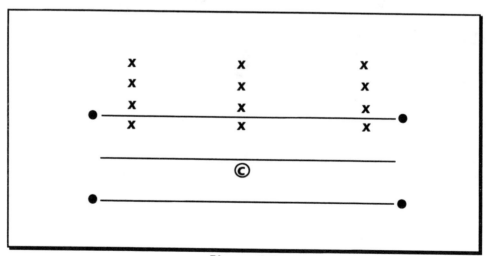

Diagram 8-2

Drill 8-3: Crossover Lateral Run

Objective: To warm-up; to improve the ability to run laterally.

Equipment needed: None.

Description: The players spread out in three lines facing the coach. Using a hand signal, the coach directs the players to run laterally (as opposed to shuffling) until he commands them to stop. On the command "defend", the players come to a halt and assume their proper defensive position. After a predetermined number of lateral runs, the coach signals the players to spring past him as fast as they can.

Coaching points:
- The players should keep their shoulders square to the line on which they are running laterally at all times.
- Proper body positioning (i.e. hips, arms, head, etc.) should be emphasized at all times during the drill.
- Players should move up one yard in front of the cones.

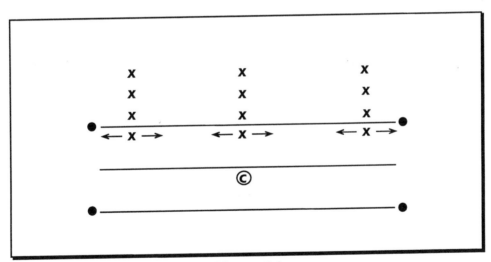

Diagram 8-3

Drill 8-4: Lateral Slide

Objective: To warm-up; to improve the ability to move laterally.

Equipment needed: None.

Description: The players spread out in three lines facing the coach. Using a hand signal, the coach directs the players to laterally slide one step in the direction he pointed. They then come to a complete stop and assume their proper defensive stance. Next, the coach again signals for the players to laterally slide one step either in the same or the opposite direction. After a predetermined number of slides, the coach then points straight ahead to signal the players to sprint as fast as they can past him.

Coaching points:
- The drill can be modified to require the players to continue to slide laterally until told to stop before they assume their defensive stance.
- The coach should emphasize that the players should maintain proper body positioning at all times during the drill.
- Players should move up one yard in front of the cones.

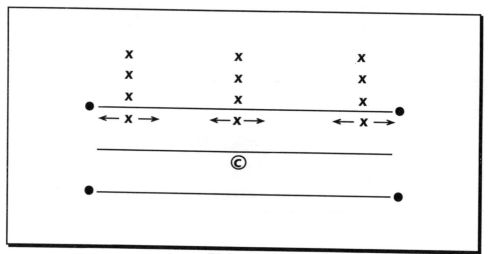

Diagram 8-4

CHAPTER 9

Blueprint for Success

Football coaches vary in a variety of obvious ways—appearance, coaching philosophy, coaching style, mannerisms, etc. In at least one important area, however, successful football coaches share one fundamental characteristic—each has a blueprint for success that he would attribute as the basis for his positive achievements as a coach. While some variation undoubtedly exists between the elements that comprise the various blueprints for success within the football coaching community, it can be argued that most— if not all—of the following ten items would be included on the blueprint list of every successful coach:

1. **Be motivated.** All successful football coaches share a passion for the game. A football coach should love what he does. He must assume a positive attitude toward his job.

2. **Be yourself.** A football coach should establish his own identity and style. While he may emulate other individuals in the field, he should not imitate them. He should work within his own personal parameters to be successful. He should deal with others in a sincere manner. At the beginning of a practice season, he should tell his players about his own mannerisms and ways of expressing himself. For example, a coach may state "that was a pretty good job," when he may mean "that was *real good*."

3. **Be organized.** All successful football coaches are organized. Seldom is anything of importance left to chance. Responsibilities and duties are identified. Priorities are established. All stones should be turned over.

4. **Be prepared.** Successful football coaches have a well-thought out plan for dealing with likely situations—both on the field and off. They have the foresight to prepare for every reasonable contingency.

5. **Be decisive.** Successful football coaches avoid indecision at all times. In almost every situation, they are able to make important decisions quickly and firmly. Fear of failure does not inhibit their ability to reason and then act accordingly.

6. ***Be focused.*** Successful football coaches are able to devote their energies to the task at hand. By concentrating on coaching and avoiding distractions, they are better able to perform their job in a professional and competent manner.

7. ***Be honest.*** A successful coach is a man of his word. He is a man of his word in all things. Dishonesty—for whatever reason—sows disrespect from others, as well as for himself.

8. ***Be loyal.*** A successful coach is loyal to his fellow coaches, his players, and himself (his ideals and philosophy). He treats others with respect. He believes in his colleagues and players.

9. ***Be open-minded.*** A successful coach realizes that learning is an on-going process that never ends. He actively searches for improved solutions to unsolved problems or better ways of doing things. He solicits the opinions of others. He is a good listener.

10. ***Be committed.*** A successful coach is committed to winning and to the welfare and all-around development of his players.

Above all—Don't take a good player and overcoach him—Let him do what he does best within your system.

CHAPTER 10

Glossary of Football Terms

The following terms are pertinent to defensive football players:

ARC release—The tight end or the slot receiver releases in an outside arc either to block the defensive back or to run a pass route.

Back side—The side away from which the play is directed.

Base block—The offensive lineman's head fires straight at a defender and attempts to block him in either direction.

Counter spin— Used by the nose as a change up to counter the actions of a pulling guard.

Crack-back block—Maneuver where a wide receiver angles sharply to make an inside block on a linebacker or defensive back.

Cross block—Change in assignments between two offensive linemen.

Double team —An inside lineman drive blocks the defender and the outside lineman attacks the defender from the side.

Down block—A lineman blocks to his inside on the next defender. In many cases, this player is a linebacker.

Draw—A play where a pass is faked. The offensive linemen pass block the oncoming defensive lineman to the outside, hopefully to allow the ball carrier to break between the rushing linemen.

Drop-back pass—The quarterback drops approximately straight back in an area between the offensive guards and sets up to pass.

Flex—A split taken by the tight end between two and five yards from the nearest offensive tackle.

Football position —On contact every defensive player should employ a proper football position. In this position, a player's head and eyes are up, back arched, tail low, legs spread comfortably for balance, weight on the balls of his feet, and his arms hanging loosely in front of his body. From this hitting position, a defender is ready to deliver a blow and to react quickly in any direction.

Front—Refers to the defensive linemen on the front line—defensive ends, tackles, and linebackers.

Front side—The side to which the play is directed.

Gang tackling— Maximum pursuit by the entire defensive unit in order to make contact on the ball carrier.

Hand shiver—A defensive technique in which a blow is delivered with the heels of the hands by extending the arms and locking the elbows on contact; used to keep blockers away from a defender's body and legs.

High wall—The offensive lineman's head goes inside his opponent in an attempt to turn out the defensive man.

Lead step—To step first with the foot toward the direction in which the player is going.

Log block—A block in which the pulling lineman tries to seal the defender inside.

L.O.S.— The line of scrimmage.

Motion—Extended movement by an offensive back prior to the snap of the ball.

Near back—The running back nearest a particular player.

Nerf football—A ball that is often used in those drills which do not employ an offensive center and a quarterback. Can be used by a lineman who holds onto it while assimilating a snap.

Neutral Zone—The space between the offense and the defense—typically, the length of the ball.

North—A term used to tell the defender, he is attacking up field.

Penetrate—Charge taken by a defensive man to get into the offensive backfield.

Play action pass—An offensive maneuver where a pass is thrown after faking run action.

P.O.A.—Point of attack.

Pressure key—The particular blocker that is aligned to the outside of a defender's visual key.

Pull-up pass—The quarterback moves laterally before setting up to pass inside his offensive tackles.

Pursuit—Movement to the ball at the proper angle after a defender's initial defensive responsibility has been fulfilled.

Quick block—A type of block which is used on quick passes. The offensive line fires out in an attempt to get the defenders' hands down.

Quick receiver—Any eligible pass receiver on or close to the L.O.S. (ends, wing, slot or flankers).

Reach block—A block where your visual key tries to get his head to your outside on a running play.

Rip technique—A technique used by a defensive lineman to come across the face of his visual key.

SAG—Strong side tackle aligns one yard off the L.O.S.

Scoop block—An offensive lineman reaches to the play side area, picking up any opposite jersey that shows in that area.

Seat roll—A move that can be employed by any defensive lineman who is getting double teamed.

Skate—A shuffling technique where a defensive lineman's outside foot is kept back and his shoulders square to the L.O.S. to prevent being hooked.

Skin—A technique used by a defender to get to the outside of his visual key.

Slotback—A back who takes his position approximately one yard behind the L.O.S., between the split end and tackle.

Spin—A move that can be employed by any defensive lineman to avoid a double team block or a down block by the pressure key.

Split end—An end who splits five yards or more outside the tackle.

Sprint-out pass—The quarterback moves laterally outside his offensive tackle before passing or running.

Strong side—The side of the formation which has the most number of players.

Throwback pass—An offensive maneuver where the quarterback moves in one direction and then passes back in the opposite direction.

Trap—A play where a defensive player is drawn across the L.O.S and is trapped by the opposite guard.

Visual key—the player you are looking at-generally the player you align on.

Weak side—The side of the formation with the fewest number of players.

Wingback—A back who takes his position one yard behind the L.O.S. and three yards or less outside the tight end.

All successful football coaches share a passion for the
game.

About the Authors

Denny A. Marcin

Denny Marcin has enjoyed great success during his 33 years of coaching football defenses. Marcin served on the gridiron staff of the University of North Carolina—first as the defensive coordinator (1978-1986) and then as the assistant head coach (1987-1988). During his tenure, UNC placed 24 defensive players in the NFL, including all-time N.F.L. great Lawrence Taylor. As Assistant Head Football Coach and Defensive Coordinator (1988-1996) at the University of Illinois, Marcin helped lead Illinois to six postseason bowl appearances and one Big 10 Championship. In the process, Marcin coached the Big 10's top defense in 1994 and second best defense in 1995. Marcin currently resides in Champaign, Illinois with his wife of 32 years, Betsey. He and Betsey have four children; sons—Jeff and Denny, daughter-in-law Lynn, daughters —Melinda and Susan, and grandson Carlton.

James A. Peterson, Ph.D.

James A. Peterson, Ph.D., is a free-lance writer who resides in Mesa, Arizona. A 1966 graduate of the University of California at Berkley, Peterson served on the faculty of the United States Military Academy at West Point for 16 years. A prolific writer, Peterson has written or co-authored 43 books and more than 150 published articles. A Fellow of the American College of Sports Medicine, he has appeared on several national television shows, including ABC's Good Morning America, The CBS Evening News, ABC's Nightline, and The Home Show. He and his wife, Susan, have been married for over 28 years.

ADDITIONAL FOOTBALL RESOURCES FROM

■ **COACHING LINEBACKERS**
by Jerry Sandusky and Cedric X. Bryant
1996 ■Paper■ 136 pp
ISBN 1-57167-059-9 ■ $15.00

■ **COACHING OFFENSIVE BACKS**
by Steve Axman
1997 ■Paper■ 230 pp
ISBN 1-57167-088-2 ■ $19.00

■ **DEVELOPING AN OFFENSIVE GAME PLAN**
by Brian Billick
1997 ■Paper■ 102 pp
ISBN 1-57167-046-7 ■ $15.00

■ **101 DEFENSIVE FOOTBALL DRILLS
(3 VOLUMES)**
by Bill Arnsparger and James A. Peterson
1997 ■Paper■ 128 pp■ $15.00 each
Vol #1, ISBN 1-57167-063-7
Vol #2, ISBN 1-57167-064-5
Vol #3, ISBN 1-57167-065-3

TO PLACE YOUR ORDER:
U.S. customers call
TOLL FREE (800)327-5557,
or write
COACHES CHOICE Books, P.O. Box 647, Champaign, IL 61824-0647,
or FAX: (217) 359-5975